HERITAGE BAKING

HERITAGE BAKING

Recipes for Rustic Breads and Pastries Baked with Artisanal Flour from Hewn Bakery

by ELLEN KING

with Amelia Levin

Photographs by John Lee

CHRONICLE BOOKS
SAN FRANCISCO

Library of Congress Cataloging-in-Publication Data

Names: King, Ellen, author. | Levin, Amelia, author. | Hewn Bakery.
Title: Heritage baking / by Ellen King of Hewn Bakery with Amelia Levin ; photographs by John Lee.
Description: San Francisco : Chronicle Books, [2018] | Includes bibliographical references and index.
Identifiers: LCCN 2018009826 | ISBN 9781452167879 (hardcover : alk. paper)
Subjects: LCSH: Bread. | Baking. | Grain. | Heirloom varieties (Plants) | LCGFT: Cookbooks.
Classification: LCC TX769 .K557 2018 | DDC 641.81/5—dc23
LC record available at https://lccn.loc.gov/2018009826

Manufactured in China.

Designed by Supriya Kalidas & Alice Chau

Photographs by John Lee
Illustrations by Hannah Ross
Prop styling by Emma Star Jensen

10 9 8 7 6 5 4 3 2 1

Chronicle Books LLC
680 Second Street
San Francisco, California 94107
www.chroniclebooks.com

TO ASHER

my VP of tasting and the reason for Hewn

Hewn *adjective* \hyün\
1. cut or shaped by striking forcibly with an ax, sword, or other cutting instrument; chopped; hacked, as used in colonial times to describe hand-hewn beams. **2.** made, shaped, smoothed, with cutting blows, as in to hew a statue

HEWN
CLOSED

CONTENTS

Country Pan Loaf
$9.15
Country Cheddar
$7.50
Polenta
Pumpkin Se
$7.50
Midwest Blend
$9.50
Country
$6.50

INTRODUCTION

The crust—crunchy and slightly dusty—crackles between your teeth. The crumb, with its many irregular holes, is spongy to the bite. Good bread is airy, not at all dry, and light, but also rich, satisfying, and soulful.

"WOW," I HEAR PEOPLE SAY when they try our bread for the first time. "This is real bread." I'm not trying to pat myself on the back by sharing this. I am paying homage to the farmers and artisan millers we work with every day to make bread and baked goods from sustainably grown grain. We wouldn't exist as a bakery without them. It's their flavorful, nutritious flours and grains that make our breads and pastries delicious.

This book is the story of Hewn, my bakery, and of the heritage baking we do there and at home. Here you'll find recipes for our favorite breads, cookies, galettes, and other treats we've developed to spotlight the fresh, local flours that are, thankfully, becoming more available to bakers everywhere, wherever you are. This story is also about migration, agriculture, and how we eat in America—and it all starts with wheat.

In recent years, more people have been diagnosed with celiac disease and other dietary intolerances and sensitivities. As such, wheat has become a symbol of gastrointestinal distress. But wheat is also a symbol of hope. We hope that small-scale farmers of sustainable grains are able to reverse 150 years of industrialization and monoculture to bring back the beautiful biodiversity and flavors of the wheat and flours of our ancestors.

These days, with the proliferation of farmers' markets across the country, many of us can easily differentiate between a candy-like heirloom tomato grown just a handful of miles away and the mealy beefsteaks lining grocery store bins. When our customers try our heritage breads and pastries, they can likewise decipher similar nuances in wheat flours, from the nutty and creamy flavor of Red Fife to the caramel flavors of a Turkey Red to the earthy punch of Marquis.

Today, many Americans shop for organic and sustainably grown fruits and vegetables, humanely raised meat, and even biodynamic wines. Knowing that, it's curious that many people purchase commodity all-purpose flour right off the store shelf without even asking where it came from, how it was milled, or how the wheat was grown.

There's a reason most of us have not tasted sustainably grown organic flour. Growing heirloom grains requires extensive land and time, partners like local millers and artisan bakers, and consumers who can increase demand. After years of seeding, sowing, and harvesting, we're just now beginning to see the growth of heritage varieties that were lost during years of rampant industrialization and commercialization.

You can mill your own sustainably grown wheat into flour at home—we offer some instructions for this on page 31—but my hope is that one day, all over the United States (and beyond!) bakers will buy their flour from local farmers and/or millers who mill wheat grown nearby, without pesticides and insecticides. When you've had freshly milled, local flour, it's really hard to go back to the commodity stuff that sits on store shelves, getting staler and blander by the day.

HOW I CAME TO BREAD

My first taste of "real" bread came while I was studying in Norway and traveling to European countries during college. The bread was rustic, hearty, and best of all—especially for a student—cheap. As a midwesterner who had grown up in the suburbs of Chicago, I had never tasted bread like that.

A few years later, when I was a graduate student in American history at the University of Maine, I learned more about organic farming from the Common Ground Country Fair, an annual gathering highlighting the agricultural traditions and history of Maine. This experience inspired me to research culinary history from the colonial times. I learned about what colonists and Native Americans ate, how they grew and produced their food, and the impact these cuisines had on our country. I would even read through old farm journals to learn about the changing landscape of the country's terrain.

Somewhere along the way, my goal of becoming a professor faded away, and it was time for me to get a "real" job and start paying off my student loans. I moved to Seattle after graduate school and landed a job at a tech company. It paid well and allowed me to travel, but it wasn't something I was passionate about. Two years into this job, September 11th happened. I was in Florida for a business trip and wound up staying there for almost two weeks until I could get a flight back home. During that time, I had an epiphany: Life was too short to work at an unfulfilling job. It was time for me to follow my true passions for cooking and baking.

It was a year until I would be able to enroll at the Seattle Culinary Academy, but it was worth the wait. For the next eight years, I worked in some of the best kitchens in Seattle. I interned at a fine French restaurant run by acclaimed chef Thierry Rautureau for close to three years. It was super-intense, but I learned so much from that experience. Later, I went on to work for chef Andrew Will at Carmelita, an upscale vegetarian restaurant in Seattle that has since closed.

Through all of this, there was great bread. In Seattle, I was exposed to produce from farms just a few miles away, and I discovered the beauty of delicious, sourdough-style artisan breads. I learned about the origins of flour, and I connected with farmers in eastern Washington who were growing heritage varieties of wheat. I became obsessed with naturally fermented breads. All of this would come in handy later on.

I was also fortunate to spend time at Quillisascut Farmstead Cheese School in Rice, Washington, about an hour and a half north of Spokane.

Quillisascut is no ordinary cheese-making school; it's also a sustainable farm. While I was there, I milked goats, butchered chickens and sheep, and harvested produce from the garden. When I came back to Seattle, I talked my way into the artisan cheese buyer job at Whole Foods, during which I sourced distinctive and exceptional cheese selections from Oregon, California, and Washington state. I was enjoying the world of food and started to ponder my next steps professionally.

Then I had a baby. Asher was born two months early, in December 2006, and everything changed. After a difficult pregnancy and delivery, I had a premature newborn to care for. Soon after Asher's birth, my former partner was offered a job in Chicago and we made a decision to move back to the Midwest. Shortly thereafter, my father died suddenly of a heart attack. I felt as if my world had imploded. We went from a beautiful house in Seattle looking out at Mt. Rainier to a small condo in Evanston. I didn't know anyone in our new town. I missed Seattle—the outdoors, the food, and of course, the bread. I was tired and probably a little depressed.

That year, my mom gave me Chad Robertson's *Tartine Bread* cookbook for Christmas. The timing was perfect. Suffering from "bread withdrawal," I was consumed by reading the book and learning how to make bread. My life revolved around taking care of Asher and baking bread.

I started collecting every cookbook I could find about bread and baking. I made my own starter and drove to Indiana for fifty-pound bags of organic flour, since it was one of the few places that sold direct to home cooks. I kept my house warmer in the winter and colder in the summer to maintain the perfect proofing conditions.

When I fed Asher, I would also feed the starter sitting on my counter. When I put him down for a nap, I would get as much of the dough mixing done as I could manage. I knew I had about two hours to complete the mixes. When Asher woke up, I would shape the bread while he played. I found that using my hands, eyes, ears, and nose all at once—as you must when baking bread—was incredibly calming and fulfilling.

Soon, we were overwhelmed by all the loaves I was baking, so I started selling some to the families at my son's preschool. This became the Underground Bread Club. To deliver the bread, I would load up the Burley trailer on my bicycle with my then three-year-old son, Asher, and plop all of the wrapped loaves on top of him. I would bike all around Evanston, and Asher would run the bread to the doors and collect the money while I stayed with the bike to fend off the crazy, bread-hungry squirrels. Sometimes, I loaded up his backpack with loaves and he would exchange the bread for cash at preschool. So maybe I'm not super-proud of that delivery method, but one thing's for sure: Providing bread to all of the parents and others in the neighborhood connected us in an amazing, unspoken way.

THE BIRTH OF HEWN

Opening the bakery was a huge undertaking but well worth the risk and hard work. Hewn brought my passion to an even higher level, one that's helped myself, my immediate family, and hopefully many others.

In the summer of 2012, one of the mothers in the Underground Bread Club—Julie Matthei—asked me if I ever thought about opening a bakery. My immediate answer? Absolutely not! I

MATADOR
HEWN

KITTERY
OPEN

knew that if I opened a retail bakery, I would never have a life. But the more that I thought about it, I realized the timing was right. Asher was getting ready to start kindergarten, and I had been baking bread for two and a half years. I didn't want to do anything else except bake and I clearly couldn't keep doing it out of my home kitchen.

One August day, Julie and I went to a Cubs game. This was before the Cubs were good, so we had a lot of time to talk. We started hashing out an idea for opening a bakery. Five months later, in December 2013, Julie and I formed a limited liability corporation. Six months later, we opened Hewn. Looking back on it, we really had no idea what we were doing nor what to expect. At first, our plan was to be open three days a week, sell thirty to forty loaves of bread, and close after selling out. But once we wrote our business plan, we realized that we needed to sell more than just bread, so we started to offer sandwiches, sweets, and pastries, too.

From the beginning, we relied on our steadfast partner in bread, Justin Holmes, to help us steer the ship. Befitting the old-fashioned nature of the bakery, our mothers, who knew each other from their knitting group, introduced Justin to me. Justin was working at a bakery in Oregon, and when he came to Chicago for a family reunion, I offered to meet him at the airport. I picked him up, took him to lunch, and told him about the bakery I wanted to open. Within four months, Justin uprooted his life and moved to Evanston to help open the bakery. For the past five years, Justin has helped lead the team of bakers who have made Hewn a success. I am incredibly grateful to him for his hard work, dedication, and consistently steady presence amid all of the moving parts that keep the bakery going strong.

Through all of this, I have leaned on Julie's calm, sensible nature; she is the "rock" of our bakery. Over time, we morphed from business partners to partners in life as well, sharing a commitment to each other and to the bakery. I have also leaned heavily on our amazing team. Many bakers I know—including myself—can be guilty of getting too set in our ways, but our bakers are very creative and flexible. They are always open to trying new things and taking on new challenges. They also share my passion about sourcing the freshest, most delicious heritage whole-wheat flour we can find.

FINDING THE WHEAT

Even before opening Hewn, I knew that if I was going to open a bakery, I had to use organic or sustainably grown wheat. I had no interest in using conventional wheat, which is tasteless and stripped of all its natural nutrients. I just didn't feel good working with it. It would be like a chef at a fine restaurant sourcing produce from industrial farms.

Since Hewn is a "real" business, I no longer need to drive fifty miles to pick up sacks of flour because farmers and artisan millers deliver them to me. At Hewn, we work with several different farmers and millers in Illinois and Wisconsin. Meadowlark Organics (see page 168), owned and operated by a family in Wisconsin, helps us source our spelt, rye, and Red Fife wheat flours. We obtain Rouge de Bordeaux wheat, grown in Montana, which is used in all of our breads. Harold Wilken (see page 190), a family farmer in Illinois, grows our Turkey Red, Glenn, Warthog, and buckwheat. He also recently built two stone-ground mills. For the first time in decades, this allows consumers near Chicago access to locally stone-ground wheat varieties on a larger scale.

I also struck up a friendship with heritage corn and barley farmer Andy Hazzard (page 106) at Chicago's Good Food Festival in 2013. I asked her if she would be willing to grow a heritage variety of wheat for us to use at Hewn. She took on the challenge and found a handful of Marquis wheat seeds to use for the project. The initial planting was 2.2 pounds, and the plot was so small that we actually used scissors to harvest the wheat for the first year! Three years later, the successful Marquis wheat crop yielded about three thousand pounds of flour. Growing heirloom grains and baking the heritage way certainly takes time and effort, but it's worth it—and not just because of the taste.

The historic origins of the word *hewn* suggest something made by hand. Perhaps, then, no other word better describes what we do at the bakery. Every day, we work hard to create something delicious and nutritious, cutting and shaping the dough by hand, with minimal equipment, the way our ancestors baked years ago.

I am a classically trained chef, but a self-taught baker. You, too, can learn to bake as I do, but you also have another important mission—to seek out and build the demand for heritage wheat. In recent years, our society has come to value heirloom vegetables and humanely raised meat. We can focus attention on the sourcing and quality of wheat, too. But it's up to you to seek out and connect with farmers and millers in your community. Hopefully this group will continue to grow.

It's also up to you to learn as much as you can about wheat farming and milling. As a history student, I've found that if we learn more about our past, we can understand the present. Only then can we work together to create a better future, not just for artisan bread bakers, sustainable grain farmers, and millers, but for all consumers and families.

THE ESSENCE OF HERITAGE BAKING

At Hewn, we define heritage baking in the following manner:

1 The use of heritage, heirloom grains that are grown sustainably (without the use of herbicides and pesticides or other chemical inputs) and freshly stone-milled.

2 The use of a natural, sourdough-style starter rather than commercial instant yeast. Unlike instant yeast, natural starters (also commonly called levain, sourdough, or "mothers") are made from wild yeast and help coax out the complex flavors of heritage wheat varieties. They also add moisture, tenderness, and even natural "preservatives" that change the pH so breads can stay fresh longer. Heritage breads don't have as long of a shelf life as grocery store commercial loaves, but you'll eat them too quickly to even notice. Natural starters also add healthy bacteria, just like a wild culture adds healthy bacteria to yogurt and butter, which helps improve gut health. Natural starters also introduce that tangy taste that makes sourdough bread so addicting.

The downside to natural starters? Making one requires a commitment—you have to keep it alive by regularly feeding it. Just like a pet, you even have to think about what you're going to do with it when you go on vacation (don't worry, I share a trick for this in chapter 1).

The good news is that heritage baking requires nothing but some workspace, a heavy-duty

ceramic or cast-iron pot, and an oven. The most important ingredients for making heritage breads are fresh flour, filtered water, salt, and lots of time and patience. I also recommend using local stone-milled flour, which will give your bread more complex flavors that are unique to your region.

Finding locally grown and milled flours in your region is not as difficult as you may think. I would first visit your local farmers' markets to see if any sustainable grain farmers are selling freshly milled wheat flour. While I support working with artisan millers, you can also buy whole wheat berries from farmers' markets, if available, and mill them yourself using special equipment (see page 31). You can search for regional flour online as well. There's nothing wrong with having bags of freshly milled flour shipped to you! Try a few different types out and choose the ones you like best.

Another idea is to call a local artisan bakery and see from where they source their flour. Some bakeries (including Hewn) even sell artisan flour directly to customers.

NOT ALL GLUTEN IS BAD

We had a gluten-free customer cautiously try our Turkey Red whole-wheat bread one day. She came back later crying tears of joy because she was able to digest and enjoy real bread. Some physicians send their gluten-sensitive patients to us because we make bread they can actually eat. We're hoping that this cookbook will help anyone make their own healthy, delicious bread.

For a few years now, we've been told to simply avoid bread completely, or at least eat it sparingly, if we want to have a healthier, gluten-free, or limited-gluten lifestyle. There are a few theories floating out there regarding the increase in gluten sensitivity. Approximately 1 percent of the United States population suffers from celiac disease, according to the National Celiac Association, but some studies suggest that close to 30 percent of people avoid gluten in their diets. This is likely due to people feeling bloated, uncomfortable, and lethargic after eating too much bread. Some scientists and theorists point to the nature of wheat itself as the culprit for our issues with gluten, while others believe it's the way modern-day wheat is grown and used. A report by Olga Oksman in the March 23, 2016, issue of the *Guardian* quotes Alessio Fasano, director of the Center for Celiac Research at Massachusetts General Hospital, saying that the "sourdough process may increase tolerance for consuming bread." According to Peter Green, director of the Celiac Disease Center at Columbia University, "The long fermentation process to make sourdough bread the old-fashioned way does reduce some of the toxic parts of gluten for those that react to it."

Additionally, when we eat anything made with commodity flour—the commonplace, nonorganic, bleached white flour found on supermarket shelves—we also ingest the herbicides, pesticides, and insecticides used to grow and store the product. Our bodies have every right to react to toxic and foreign substances. Maybe it's not the gluten but the chemicals in the flour that are creating the medical issues associated with eating bread.

Aside from the improvements in taste and texture, a huge advantage of using a natural starter is it that it starts breaking down the gluten in the flour before we ingest it, so that the gluten has already been partially "digested" before it enters our gut. When we eat bread made with commercial yeast, it speeds up the process and lessens the fermentation time. As such, the problems that can arise from eating gluten intensify.

Throughout this book, we talk a lot about "heritage" wheats, which the small-scale grain farming and artisan baking community defines as heirloom varieties with origins from all over the world. These wheats fell out of favor in the United States during the commoditization of wheat and flour. Compared with modern wheat varieties, which were bred during a time of rampant, industrial agricultural growth, heritage wheats have naturally lower levels of gluten. As a result, they need to be worked using a light hand and a gentle no-knead folding process. Overworking the dough in the form of overmixing or kneading will create a bread that's too tough and chewy, rather than tender and toothsome.

FROM FIELD TO FLOUR: HERITAGE WHEAT "TERROIR"

There's another thing about heritage wheat and baking, and this is a big one. By now you might have tried single-origin coffee from a local roaster. Have you ever noticed how you can really taste the different undertones of flavor, from blueberry to caramel and even cinnamon? Similar to wine, chocolate, and cheese, coffee beans come from distinct places with distinct weather patterns, growing seasons, soil changes, and more—all of which affect their individual taste and terroir. The same factors apply to wheat. Different varieties of wheat grow well in different regions. For example, the varieties that flourish in the Northeast may not do well in the Pacific Northwest. At Hewn, we choose flours based on what farmers are growing and milling in our region, but also on the nuanced taste and texture each variety of wheat produces when used in baking. Some are great for hearty, rustic breads, while others work better for lighter breads and baked goods.

We love Turkey Red for our rustic whole-wheat loaves, for example, because it's a hearty wheat with an earthy and caramelized taste that produces a tender crumb. It also pairs incredibly well in a muffin that's sweetened with dried fruit.

We love getting our hands on freshly milled Red Fife, which has a slightly milder taste than the Turkey Red. And our latest obsession, a flour milled from Rouge de Bordeaux, has a sharpness to it that brings out the sourdough notes, but also takes on a warm, rich flavor when paired with dark chocolate. Regional flour also infuses a little nuttiness and more complex flavors beyond just butter and sugar when used in cookies and other baked goods.

When we baked our first loaves with a locally sourced stone-milled whole wheat, I thought someone accidentally dumped cinnamon in the bread mix; it turns out that a type of rock in the soil the wheat was grown in causes that flavor. I worried our customers would hate it, but they ended up thinking it was really interesting. This is the beauty of sourcing local heritage wheat.

DEFINING HERITAGE WHEAT

The official definition of heritage wheat remains a subject of debate, but most agronomists define it as varieties that were grown in the United States before World War II. At that time, synthetic fertilizers and other chemical-laden inputs were introduced to grow crops on a much wider scale in order to feed the growing masses.

Landrace wheat is a label given to heritage varieties that have grown in a region for decades—even hundreds of years—and have adapted to the region's environment. The term *landrace* in general refers to a domesticated variety of animal species or plants that have developed over time through adaptation to the natural environment and with or without agricultural inputs.

Before industrialized wheat became more commonplace in the mid-1900s, many heritage varieties were selected in the fields by smaller farmers for the specific traits they wanted. Some varieties were grown for their flavor and bread-baking ability. Others were grown because they could withstand harsher winters and had higher yields. A few wheat varieties could grow as tall as a person. But even though tall wheat blocked out weed growth, it became more vulnerable in the fields, as storms can tip over wheat stalks.

After World War II, a dwarfing gene was added to wheat to help the crops grow shorter. This helps them better stand up to harsh weather conditions. But shorter stalks meant the wheat competed with weeds for the nutrients in the soil, so herbicides, fertilizers, and insecticides were added to the fields to ensure the wheat would outcompete the weeds and pests.

This was during the height of the Green Revolution in the United States, a time when agricultural production was ramping up fast thanks to the widening use of synthetic fertilizers on farms across the country. Whereas in the past, thousands of wheat varieties naturally adapted to their region, the Green Revolution spurred the narrowing of this selection through large-scale inbreeding to create a more uniform wheat-growing standard and more consistent yields. Modern heritage varieties came about after the 1960s by breeding heritage varieties with newer strains favored for their yield. As a result, today there are only a handful of commodity (modern) wheat varieties that are grown by conventional wheat farms. Also, conventional farms source seed from large seed companies that cannot save seeds. Seed saving is vital for heirloom varieties and held sacred by many cultures. Once, more than 19,000 wheat varieties grew around the world.

It's important to note that heritage wheat differs from ancient wheat—the group that includes biblical grains like einkorn, emmer, and spelt—which many people favor regardless of their region. These varieties have been grown for several thousand years in all parts of the world. They were the basis for some of the heritage wheat breeds that came later. While we use some of these grains in our baking at Hewn, our focus is on heritage wheats.

One of these heritage varieties was introduced to Central America and the western United States by the Spaniards, who grew wheat for the wafers used in Catholic communion and related religious ceremonies. Over the years, immigrants from other parts of Europe and the Fertile Crescent, which includes modern-day Iraq, Syria, Lebanon, Cyprus, Jordan, Israel, Palestine, Egypt, and parts of Turkey and Iran, brought with them their own strains of the crop. These strains coexisted with wheat strains already here, and were eventually bred together either by accident or on purpose.

TRAINS AND GRAINS: THE HISTORY OF HERITAGE WHEAT IN THE MIDWEST

Our bakery lies in the heart of where the modern grain economy initially took hold. The prairie around Chicago held incredible promise and potential for farmers. They built their lives around natural ponds, streams, rivers, and waterways and along edges of rolling hills and forests in order to create a diverse microcosm where they could easily grow grains, vegetables, and corn in a symbiotic fashion to feed their families and communities.

However, as more immigrant farmers settled in this region in the early 1800s, getting their product to market started to become a more laborious and even risky endeavor. The logistics were not ideal; they could either get their grains and crops to the city via horse and buggy, or send sacks of shipments on barges downstream through rivers and creeks. Once at their final destination, be it Chicago or farther down the Mississippi River in Saint Louis or New Orleans, these heavy sacks of grains had to be hauled through city streets and into buildings on the backs of migrant workers. It wasn't long before merchants realized this was a sweat-inducing, costly, and very inefficient method of distribution.

Complicating matters further, the farmers who owned these products were not able to retrieve any money for the grains until they made it to the buyer. This could take weeks or months. If any sacks fell off a barge in transit or otherwise went missing, the farmer absorbed the loss. There were no phone or telegraph lines at the time, so prices could plummet by the time the grain reached a buyer, and there was no way for farmers to know how much they would actually earn.

But, after 1830, a series of events made farming and milling grain less complicated.

- **1831** / Cyrus McCormick invents the mechanical reaper that harvests grain.
- **1837** / John Deere invents the steel plow, or prairie breaker, which allowed farmers to plow their fields more efficiently. It became easier to clear the wild, harsh, and tall grasses of the prairies to create farmland, which made it more attractive for farmers in other parts of the world to immigrate to the United States.
- **1848** / Robert C. Bristol builds the first steam-powered grain elevator, which could store grains from several different farms all at once.
- **1848** / Construction is completed on the new Galena and Chicago railroad line, the Chicago Board of Trade is established, and Chicago acquires a grain elevator and telegraph.
- **1856** / The Chicago Board of Trade designates three categories of wheat, establishing a wheat grading system.
- **1880** / John Stevens invents the roller mill.
- **1930 to 1960** / The Green Revolution spurs new agricultural growth in America, also compromising the individuality of heritage wheat and grain farmers across the United States, leading to the more uniform, commercially produced product we now know simply as flour.
- **1970** / Glyphosate is discovered, and its use as the popular weed-killer Roundup begins.

TODAY'S HERITAGE WHEAT MOVEMENT

Two simultaneous forces seem to have helped today's heritage wheat movement gain steam:

1 Consumers are seeking a deeper connection with farmers, as part of their growing desire to know where their food comes from.

2 A desire to eat "real" bread and baked goods without worrying about gluten sensitivities, starchy aftereffects, and ingesting chemicals and other unnecessary additives.

As the demand for these types of breads and baked goods grows around the country, it has become our mission as bakers to source the best ingredients we can find, just as chefs have been doing for years as part of the farm-to-table movement and the explosion of farmers' markets, urban gardens, and more. Likewise, the heritage baking movement starts with supporting our local grain farmers and artisan millers.

Growing wheat the sustainable way is a colossal task. Farmers have to plant acres and acres of grains to yield a few hundred pounds of flour, and it can be really costly—for the farmer, miller, and baker—to grow, mill, and buy this type of flour.

Case in point: It took Andy Hazzard (see page 106) three years to replenish the seed stock of Marquis wheat before she was able to cultivate enough to mill into flour and use in our breads. At the time of writing this book, we harvested the third year of this crop and finally have a few hundred pounds of Marquis with which to bake. Thankfully, we're seeing more farmers experimenting with different varieties of wheat side by side so that if one crop fails in a season, there's another one to take its place.

At Hewn, by buying grain and heritage wheat directly from local mills and farmers, we're hoping to make it economically viable for them to continue their passion and work. It's my hope that learning about the history of our country's most important crop will encourage you to discover who might be growing heirloom wheat varieties in your own area.

Some say the heritage wheat movement unofficially began in Skowhegan, Maine, one of the breadbaskets of America and not far from where I studied history. The first-ever Kneading Conference in 2007 brought together artisan bakers and small farmers, and even spurred the development of the region's first stone-ground mill. Meanwhile, on the West Coast, scientists, farmers, millers, and other experts have been working together to study and inspire the spread of sustainable grain production and milling across the country. In the Willamette Valley of Oregon, farmer Tom Hunton, fed up with the challenges of getting his wheat custom-milled, built his own mill. His Camas Country Mill, near Eugene, was the first stone mill in the region in eighty years.

In the Midwest, we've been having our own heritage wheat movement. Many formerly conventional farmers have switched to organic methods, and that includes swapping out chemical-laden cornfields for fields of sustainably grown, herbicide-free wheat, reviving different heritage varieties that were lost as commoditization took hold. Some of those farmers invested in stone mills to grind their beautiful wheat berries, and then connected with bakers like myself to help produce true artisan bread.

All this didn't happen overnight, of course. After five generations of herbicide, pesticide, and insecticide treatment, it took years for a self-declared recovering conventional farmer

like Harold Wilken (see page 190) to bring back the nutrition in his farm's soil before he could even begin organic planting. It was three more years before the first of his heritage Turkey Red, Glenn, and Warthog wheat could be harvested and used for flour and cooking. He says it's worth it to grow healthy, nutritious, beautiful-tasting food that we can safely eat and enjoy.

Seed-saving programs, both federally sanctioned and privately operated, are key to the continued growth of heritage grains in this country. As large-scale wheat breeding increased in the early 1900s, and was controlled less and less by small farmers, industrial breeders would select certain heritage varieties and reject others based on their goals for higher-protein, higher-yield wheat. These so-called modern wheats, typically grown with the aid of pesticides, insecticides, and genetic management, are less subject to disease and weather-related destruction than heritage varieties. However, that's beginning to change. As farmers like Andy Hazzard select the heritage varieties with the best traits and characteristics for their immediate, climate-specific region, we're seeing less of a need for crossbreeding, spraying, and other artificial enhancements.

In just a couple of years, Hazzard's Marquis wheat—which she selected specifically for its hardy nature and ability to withstand harsher weather like that in northern Illinois—has flourished. Not only was it the best variety to plant in her location, but the plant itself really took root and adapted to its environment. Each season, she continues to save the best seeds, which have flourished the most, using those to sow her crop the following year. Fortunately, she's not the only American working to restore the biodiversity of these heritage varieties. The USDA's gene bank has hundreds of thousands of heritage and modern wheat seeds available for experimentation. Sure, these packets contain a mere 5 g of seed each, but to see Hazzard's handful of Marquis seeds blossom over a few years with some extra-special TLC is truly inspiring.

THE ART AND CRAFT OF STONE-GROUND MILLING

The cultivation of heritage wheat can't exist without mills. The idea that flour is a shelf-stable product was ingrained into us from the time we were little kids helping our parents and grandparents bake in the kitchen. The idea of buying whole-wheat berries at a farmers' market and milling them ourselves, or buying freshly milled grains from an artisan mill, is still very new. Even several years after opening Hewn, it still feels unusual. That's because these heritage flours have not been available to us—until now. Thankfully, small farmers, millers, bakers, and other passionate players are coming together to bring back our historic tradition of growing grains and producing flour. Flour doesn't have to be a stale, cheap ingredient we use without giving it a second thought.

Stone-ground milling is both a craft and an art. If you've ever seen a miller at work, he or she must choose between a variety of screens and settings in order to achieve the perfect balance between texture (coarse versus fine) and flavor. The extraction rate—how much or little of the fiber-rich bran and flavorful, oily germ is removed in the milling process—determines what type of flour is created, from coarser whole-wheat flours used in heartier, rustic breads to lighter, sifted flours meant for buttery brioche and pastries.

Industrial roller mills simply pulverize the entire wheat berry, separating away the endosperm, bran, and germ that contribute all the flavor, character (terroir), and nutrients. Once the endosperm, bran, and germ are separated, the mill will combine back some of the bran and germ to create a "whole-wheat" flavor. Then it is heat-treated, bleached, chemically preserved, and "enriched" with processed vitamins to create a more uniform, shelf-stable, and commercial baker–friendly product. But, it's also bland, missing the richness of stone-milled flour.

Often, for products labeled *whole wheat*, some of the bran and germ has been added back to the milled white flour, but who knows where that bran and germ came from? It's as if you took Turkey Red wheat grown in Wisconsin, with its caramel notes, pulverized the berries in a roller mill, discarded the flavorful bran and oily germ, then mixed what's left with pulverized bran and germ from other types of wheat sourced from all around the country, then added it back to the white flour you created. The beautiful, oily, nutrient-dense material from the original wheat berry gets lost, as does the integrity and connection with the farm where the wheat was grown.

Stone-ground mills from Europe fell out of favor as industrialization took hold in the United States in the late 1800s. It takes a lot of wheat berries, time, and effort to make a decent amount of flour. And there is the problem of it being so perishable. When more of the oily germ is left intact, the flour will have more flavor—but it also has the potential to go rancid more quickly. If a small mill were to mill a batch of flour but not be able to sell it fast enough, it's lost, along with any potential profits.

We try to help our small millers avoid this problem by ordering what we need a couple of days ahead. We're also working out systems to pay our share up front, just as many consumers pay for CSAs, in order to make sure our millers are compensated for their work. We know we are lucky that we can source freshly milled flour, but our hope is that the more we help fuel demand, the more small millers can sell at farmers' markets, and perhaps even set up their own grain CSAs for consumers. We also sell some freshly milled flour in the retail section of our bakery. We hope to see this flour from sustainably grown wheat at more retail locations across the country, because we all deserve to have fresh flour in our homes.

Bread should be something more than what you use for a sandwich or slather with butter and jam. We should be able to source as many real, wholesome nutrients from bread as we get from the locally grown lettuce, heirloom tomatoes, farm-churned butter, and wholesome nut butters many of us seek out and appreciate. Bread can (and should be) a part of a nutritious diet, just as it was for our ancestors. Heritage baking—and stone-ground milling—is the answer.

Milling at Home

A home mill is a great tool when it's hard to find locally grown, freshly milled flour. Using a home mill is also a great way to make flour out of everything, from heritage wheat varieties to rye, millet, barley, buckwheat, corn, oats, and more, while preserving all the nutritional qualities of the flour. In fact, there are more farmers selling small bags of whole grains and wheat berries these days than there are artisan millers.

At home I use the Mockmill 200, which was developed by Wolfgang Mock, a well-known maker of European stone-ground mills. The home mill fits easily on my counter and gently grinds wheat berries, grains, pulses, and even spices when you feed the ingredients through the hopper. After grinding, a chute deposits the flour into a bowl. You can change the milling grade setting based on the type of flour you want to make.

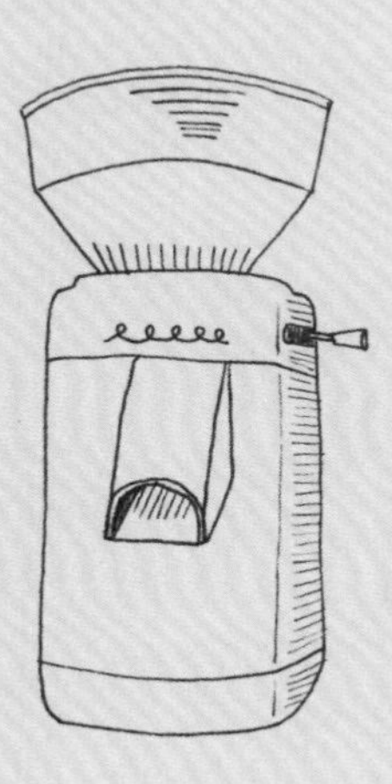

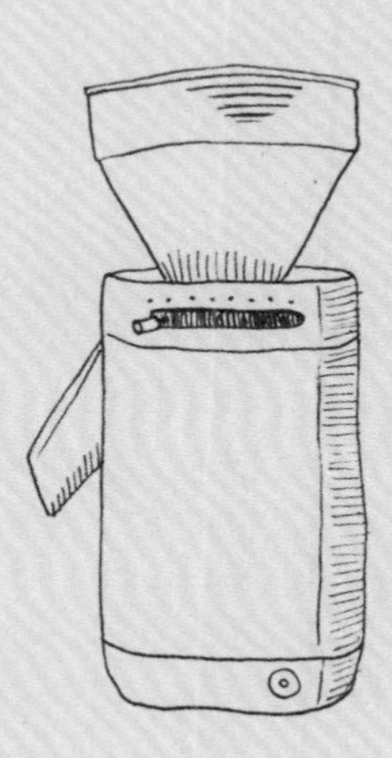

Whole wheat berries can be stored in a closed container in a dry and not too warm part of the house for months, even years. Freshly milled flour should be used within 7 to 10 days because the lack of preservatives and the oil and fat from the germ means the flour will turn stale, go rancid, and lose flavor faster than store-bought flour. You can, however, freeze the flour right away for longer-term storage, but it will go rancid if left out on the counter, just like fruit that overripens if not eaten fast enough. If you are milling your own wheat berries at home, just weigh out the grains you need for your recipe, and then mill them. Another option is to use a sifter to remove some of the bran and germ. This produces a whiter flour. There is virtually no loss of weight from milling because the entire wheat berry is used. Milling at home is also a fun activity to do with kids or even dinner party guests.

Freshly milled flour that uses the entire white berry (otherwise known as 100 percent whole-wheat or 100 percent high-extraction flour) gives breads and pastries a nutty, nougaty, complex taste and texture with all of the fiber, vitamins, and minerals still intact.

ABOUT THE RECIPES IN THIS BOOK

The most important thing before baking the bread recipes in this book is to buy a digital scale. There are many inexpensive scales on the market and they all work very well in ensuring the accuracy of your baking.

More professional and home bakers in the United States are now using a scale when they bake. In Europe, using a scale is the norm. I personally find it easier and less messy to weigh ingredients in bowls rather than using lots of cups and other measuring tools.

Baking, especially bread baking, requires precise and accurate measurements, percentages, and proportions for recipes to work. The main reason why we use only weighted measurements for our breads and lead with weights (followed by cup measurements) for our pastries is because freshly milled flours have different weights from coast to coast, bag to bag. We're not using commodity flour, which has more standardized weights across the board, so uniform cup measurements simply won't work. One cup of a hard winter wheat milled at one mill might weigh more than the same cup of a hard spring wheat because the moisture content in the flour varies from crop to crop, mill to mill.

While we highly recommend using a scale for all baking, the good thing about baking with freshly milled flour and heritage wheat is that chances are, you're going to end up with an amazing loaf of bread even if you're off by a gram here or there. So don't stress too much if you weighed 402 g flour for your starter instead of 400 g, but try not to go over (or under) on the salt.

Here's another pointer for baking with freshly milled flour: You may need to add or withhold more water when mixing dough. All stone-milled flours have different absorbtion levels. Some types can absorb more water; others require less. The wetter the dough, the easier it is for yeast to take hold and ferment the dough, give it its rise, and develop the gluten strands. Unlike commodity flour, which has more uniform moisture levels, freshly milled flour made from sustainably grown wheat varies in moisture content based on the type of wheat, the region in which it was grown, and the season when it was harvested. Moisture content might also vary based on when the wheat berries were milled. This is why we call for a reserve amount of water for all of the bread recipes in this book.

HERITAGE FLOUR, HEWN INGREDIENT, AND EQUIPMENT PRIMER

For the bread recipes in this book, we call out flours by classifications (for example, HRW or HRS), while also suggesting specific varieties like Turkey Red, Red Fife, or others. Part of the fun, we think, is exploring which heritage wheats farmers are growing and/or milling in your region. When you buy freshly milled local flour, you'll find that the taste is so distinct, so beautiful and nuanced, that it will be difficult to go back to the bagged stuff aging away on grocery store shelves.

Though we work with only a handful of heritage wheats, there are more than one hundred thousand varieties in the world. In the United States alone, thousands exist in the USDA's National Clonal Germplasm Repository (a gene bank), as well as among seed-saving farmer networks. Our goal is to continue to work with and encourage more farmers to grow these forgotten heritage, heirloom varieties so millers can mill them and we home cooks and bakers can bake with them!

After you recognize the type of wheat you want based on whether you're making bread or pastries, it's important to note the extraction rate for that particular wheat by looking at the label or talking to the farmer or miller. The extraction rate indicates how much wheat bran and germ were removed during the milling process. For example, you can have an HRW wheat that is 100 percent extraction, meaning all of the germ, bran, and endosperm remains intact—this would be a 100 percent whole-wheat flour. If you mill your grain at home and don't sift out any bran or germ, that is considered 100 percent extraction—a true whole wheat. Or you could have an HRW wheat that is 70 to 80 percent extraction, meaning 20 to 30 percent of that germ and bran has been sifted out to give the flour a slightly lighter taste and texture. The information on the extraction rate may not be readily available, but this term may pop up when you speak with your local miller or farmer. The general rule is that **the higher the extraction rate, the more the germ and the bran are present.**

In addition to the extraction rate, the number of screens the flour goes through determines the texture of the flour. Some millers refer to the use of screens as sifting—or bolting—the flour, which sounds similar but is different from what home bakers think of as sifting flour through a fine-mesh sieve.

At Hewn, we prefer to work with higher-extraction flours because we find the bran and germ of our heritage whole-wheat flours have more nuanced flavor from the local terroir as well as important nutrients. We want to hang on to every bit of these. Higher-extraction or whole-wheat breads and baked goods also have higher levels of healthy oil, fiber, and other nutrients. Our use of natural starters, gentle mixing, extra hydration, and long fermentation times help preserve that flavor. We like to use lower extraction flours for delicate pastries and baked goods.

One important fact to know about wheat is that it's seasonal. There is spring wheat and winter wheat; this refers to the growing and harvesting season of the wheat. Spring wheats are planted in March or April, depending on the region, and harvested in July or August. The primary growing regions for spring wheat are in North Dakota, South Dakota, Montana, Minnesota, eastern Washington, Oregon, southeast Idaho, and parts of Illinois and Wisconsin. Hard red spring wheat has the highest protein content—more than hard red winter wheat—and is commonly used for bread. Winter wheat production represents 70 to 80 percent of all U.S. wheat production. These varieties are planted in the fall and go dormant during the winter season. In the spring, plants resume growth and are harvested in the summer. This type of wheat is grown in areas where the winters are less frigid, such as in the Corn Belt.

It is not important to choose winter or spring. If a recipe calls for hard red winter (HRW, see right) flour and you can only find hard red spring (HRS, see below) flour, that is fine. It is more important to know first if it is hard or soft for protein content and gluten formation, and then second, whether it is red or white for flavor and the color of the finished baked product. Red flour will produce a darker looking muffin than a white wheat.

What follows is a breakdown of the types of wheat and flour grown in the United States, and the flours we work with at Hewn.

WHEAT ACRONYMS AND FLOUR TYPES

We reference the acronyms listed here in most of our recipes throughout this book. Use this glossary to help source the type of wheat you need for bread baking and some pastries in this book.

HARD RED WINTER (HRW) wheat has high protein and gluten ratios, so it's best for breads, but it can also be used like an all-purpose flour. The heritage varieties we work with include Turkey Red and Red Fife; these are mostly found in our bread recipes. This type of wheat accounts for about 40 percent of total wheat production and is grown primarily in the Great Plains (Texas, Kansas, and north through Montana).

HARD RED SPRING (HRS) wheat has high protein levels and gluten strength. This is ideal for breads and brioche doughs. Heritage varieties we use at Hewn include Turkey Red, Red Fife, Marquis, Glenn, Pfeiffer (a whole wheat derived from spelt), and Rouge de Bordeaux. HRS wheat accounts for about 20 percent of wheat production and is grown primarily in the Northern Plains (North Dakota, South Dakota, and Montana) as well as in the Midwest (Minnesota, parts of Illinois, and Wisconsin) and parts of the Northeast.

SOFT RED WINTER (SRW) wheat has lower protein and gluten levels. A high-extraction soft red flour will produce a darker-hued product. Due to the lower protein levels and lower liquid absorption, it works well as an all-purpose or pastry flour; as such, it is commonly used in the United States for cakes, cookies, and crackers. SRW wheat accounts for 15 to 20 percent of total wheat production and is grown primarily in the Pacific Northwest and also in states along the Mississippi River and in the Northeast. A variety you may find in the Northeast is Fulcaster.

SOFT RED SPRING (SRS) wheat is not as commonly grown as soft red winter. It has lower protein, a reddish hue when milled, and a buttery and nutty finish. This can be blended with a hard wheat to increase its protein. A modern heritage variety found in the midwest is Warthog.

SOFT WHITE (SW) wheat, like the soft red, has low protein and gluten levels with a naturally occurring whiter pigment. A high-extraction soft white flour will produce a product with a lighter color. Soft white flours can be either soft white winter (SWW) or soft white spring (SWS) and work well in any of the non-bread, pastry recipes in this book. At Hewn, we use Sonora or Richland, which can be either SWW or SWS, in pastry baking.

The way heritage flour is milled is very important. Milling each batch of wheat berries using a stone mill helps retain some of those flavors of terroir we talked about earlier. In a commodity roller mill, you might have bushels of wheat berries from different regions or states that are milled together. That works for commodity flour because the flour is milled to have complete uniformity and never fluctuate from the formula. That's why you'll often see small grain farmers starting to mill their own wheat, or partnering with a smaller, artisan miller who can assure them the flour produced has come strictly from their wheat.

FLOURS WE USE AT HEWN

HERITAGE WHOLE-WHEAT FLOUR (100% EXTRACTION)

We like to look at extraction rates to know how wheaty the flour will taste and the coarseness of its texture. Both hard and soft wheat flours can have 100 percent extraction, meaning that none of the bran, germ, or endosperm has been removed. Hard wheat flours are milled at higher extraction rates, so they work best in bread and hearty baked goods. Interestingly, some commodity flours labeled *whole wheat* actually strip away all of the germ and bran to get to the starchy endosperm, only to add some, but not all, of those nutrients back into the flour. This is what it means to be truly whole grain. You may find some high-extraction wheat flours with a 90 to 95 percent extraction rate, which means 5 to 10 percent of the bran and germ was removed; this type of flour also works great for bread and pastries.

Something to remember with high-extraction flour is that bread and pastries will be denser and have more compact holes because the bran and germ cut through the gluten strands like tiny razors. This is why several of the bread recipes call for some lower-extracted heritage flours so the bread will be a little lighter. You might need more hydration (water) when baking with these flours. Whole-wheat (100 percent extraction) flour also has a shorter shelf life because it contains the bran, germ, and oils that will make it go rancid quicker than highly

Hewn's Favorite Heritage Wheat Varieties

Listed here are some of the heritage varieties grown in the Midwest and in other parts of the country that we use at the bakery. We receive all of these flours freshly milled by local stone millers.

TURKEY RED (HRW/HRS, 13% PROTEIN): This wheat was first introduced in Kansas by Russian Mennonite farmers. It has since seen a revival in Kansas and other parts of the Midwest. Turkey Red can have a higher protein level, and when used in whole-wheat or high-extraction form in breads, it will impart a very rich and earthy, slightly caramelized flavor.

RED FIFE (HRW/HRS, 12% PROTEIN): This wheat has a slightly bitter, but pleasant flavor, and it brings out the sourdough notes of the starter really well. Because of the slight bitterness, this flour works best when combined with other flours. It doesn't work as well for brioche dough or other recipes where you want the end result to taste sweeter. We use this flour in our muffins, however, to introduce a rich and nutty taste.

MARQUIS (HRS, 12.5% PROTEIN): This wheat, a hybrid between Red Fife and Hard Red Calcutta, is grown locally in Illinois for us and is also grown on the East Coast and parts of the West Coast; it has a distinctly earthy flavor that makes breads more flavorful.

ROUGE DE BORDEAUX (HRS, 14% PROTEIN): A variety from France grown in the 1800s, this wheat has a rich and smooth flavor like butter. When used for bread, it will take on the sour notes from the starter, and when used for brownies and cookies, it imparts a mellow nutty wheat flavor that pairs well with chocolate without overpowering it. This flour can also be used in brioche and in any pastry recipe.

SONORA (SWS OR SWW, 11% PROTEIN): This white-colored flour has a delicate and creamy flavorful wheat taste. The lightness of the flour makes it work well in place of all-purpose or pastry flour for our pastry recipes and can be blended into some of the bread recipes, too.

GLENN (HRS, 14% PROTEIN): A modern variety bred from heritage varieties after the 1960s, this has a very mild flavor that works great for all bread recipes.

WARTHOG (HRW/SRS, 10–12% PROTEIN): This is another modern heritage variety that, because of its neutral flavor and lighter protein content, works best in any of the pastry recipes. However, because of its lower gluten levels, it is best blended with higher-protein, stronger-flavored wheats for some bread recipes using a blend of whole-wheat and sifted wheat flours.

sifted flour. Store it in your freezer if you don't plan to use it within a week or so.

SIFTED OR BOLTED HERITAGE FLOUR

This type of flour has gone through a sifting process, so it contains less of the bran and germ. It can be lighter in color, density (weight), and flavor compared with 100 percent whole-wheat flour. Think of this flour like a sifted bread flour or possibly all-purpose flour. Many artisan millers call this sifted or bolted flour because they have used screens to remove some of the bran and germ. We know this is confusing because when bakers hear the words *sifted* and *flour* used together it usually means to get out your fine-mesh strainer and sift the flour to break up clumps. You may also see farmers and artisan millers use the words *bolted flour* to describe this type of flour, which is a much older term used in the milling industry. For the purposes of this book, we refer to heritage wheat flour that is not 100 percent whole wheat as sifted heritage flour.

HERITAGE RYE FLOUR

I first discovered rye when I was studying in Norway. I ate rye bread every day and tasted a few different varieties. Rye is often used to make spirits, but fresh stone-milled rye flour also makes amazing bread. There are German, French, and Roman varieties. At Hewn, we have made bread with the "Driftless rye" from Wisconsin, but I would recommend sourcing whatever rye grows in your region. Rye actually grows like a weed and it flourishes in many regions of our country, so most likely you have access to some locally grown rye. Rye can be coarse or fine. It can also have some of the bran or germ removed to be classified as light rye, because it has been finely milled to remove more of the bran and germ, resulting in a much finer, silkier product.

SPELT

This is a heritage grain dating back several thousand years that actually is a cousin to wheat. Those who can't tolerate wheat gluten will often reach for spelt, which has a different type of gluten than other flours. The grain industry stopped producing spelt years ago because of the extra step needed in the milling process to remove the hull. When used in bread and even in cookies and pancakes, it adds a tender texture and a distinctly nutty and rich flavor. We use a spelt that has been sifted using screens with about 12 to 15 percent of the germ and bran removed. We also use Pfeiffer wheat, which is an HRS heritage flour derived from spelt.

OTHER HEWN INGREDIENTS

STONE-ROLLED OATS

Look for thick stone-rolled oats that have not been presoaked. Many people think that steel-cut oats are healthier or more nutritious, but stone-rolled oats that are made using stone grinders have the same and even more nutrient levels as steel-cut oats. At Hewn, we source a hull-less, stone-rolled oat variety from Andy Hazzard of Hazzard Free Farm (see page 106). We prefer the hull-less variety because it is never heated, which would otherwise damage the grain, leaving it bland and nutrient-poor. The raw hull-less variety is loaded with healthy, omega-3 fatty acids, and it has a delicate, smooth, and pleasantly nutty taste that is best used in any of the recipes calling for oats. It also makes a very creamy and smooth oatmeal for breakfast.

Other Common Types of Flour

NAME	EXTRACTION RATE, MILLING INFORMATION	WHEAT CLASSIFICATION	CHARACTERISTICS
WHOLE WHEAT (Protein varies)	100% extraction, contains all of the germ and bran.	HRS, HRW, SRW, SRS, or SW	Red pigment. Ideal for bread recipes.
BREAD FLOUR (High protein above 11.5%)	Bolted, sifted, a percent of bran and germ removed. Lower extraction rate.	HRS or HRW	Silkier flour, percent of bran and germ removed. Contains red pigment. Used in bread recipes.
AP FLOUR (Protein 9.5–11.5%)	Larger percentage of bran and germ removed. Lower extraction rate, could be 60–75%.	SRW, SRS, or SW or blend of HRW and HRS	Great for all sweet recipes, not as great for bread. Can be used in all muffin, scone, cookie, and brioche recipes.
PASTRY FLOUR (Protein 8–9.5%)	Less gluten, and very low extraction rates; could be 50%. Large amount of bran and germ removed.	SRW, SRS, or SW	Very fine, silky flour. Can be used in all muffins, cookies, and scone recipes.
CAKE FLOUR (Protein below 8%)	Very low extraction rates, below 50%. Large amounts of bran and germ removed.	SRW, SRS, or SW	Very fine flour, not necessary to use in any of the recipes.

SALT

When we call for salt in our recipes, we are referring to fine sea salt. Fine kosher salt is a decent substitute. Stay away from iodized salt because it can dry out and affect the delicate taste of the bread.

BUTTER

At Hewn, we prefer to use a high-fat European butter such as Plugra, but any good-quality butter will work. Just make sure it's unsalted. Using salted butter will make everything taste too salty and strip away the natural flavors of the heritage flours. Historically, salt was added to butter as a preservation technique. However, with modern refrigeration, it's added only for flavor.

SUGAR

We try to source pure cane sugar for recipes that call for sugar. The finer the granulated sugar, the better, as it will blend more thoroughly into your dough during mixing. If you source an organic sugar, it may have more caramel color, which means more of its natural elements remain intact and it is less processed. Pure, white granulated sugar goes through several processing stages to remove what commodity standards define as impurities, and this includes some of the natural coloring. Though beet sugar is another less processed, more natural sugar, we prefer cane sugar.

TURBINADO AND DEMERARA SUGARS

We use these sugars as a decorative, textural topping for some of our muffins and brioche. These are coarse sugars containing more molasses, which impart extra sweetness and caramel flavor. Their texture adds a little sugary crunch to pastries and piecrusts.

WATER

A good rule of thumb is to use filtered water in the bread recipes. Chlorinated water straight from the tap can hinder your starter from catching wild yeast in the air. For the bread recipes, the ideal water temperature ranges between 76°F and 79°F [24.5°C and 25.5°C]. Never use hot water, as it can cause the starter to "overeat." On the flip side, water that is too cold will slow down your starter production.

INSTANT YEAST

We prefer to use natural starters because they help draw out the natural flavors of our heritage whole-wheat flours better than instant yeast, which can squash those flavors in bread baking. However, we do use a little instant yeast in our brioche. We also use it occasionally in pastry recipes if we need a quick fix and don't want to use fresh yeast, which you typically need to use in larger volumes. We use instant yeast for our brioche recipe because natural starters tend to become more unpredictable during the mixing and baking process when you're introducing sugar and butter. Though it's a commercial product, we don't shun it entirely; it has its place in our bakery and most likely will in your home as well. Note, though, that we do not use active dry yeast, which requires a mixture of water to hydrate before using.

BAKING POWDER

I choose aluminum-free double-acting baking powder as the most natural and effective baking agent versus more commercial types.

HERITAGE BAKING EQUIPMENT

What's really exciting about heritage baking is that you don't need an expensive steam-injected oven or other fancy equipment and tools. Sure, there are some staples—a digital scale, bannetons, a large ceramic or cast-iron pot—but by and large the beauty of heritage baking comes from simply using quality flour, quality ingredients, a few learned techniques, and most of all, the luxury of time.

Following are the essentials for baking real bread at home. At Hewn, we call it our heritage bread-baking starter pack.

Starter Pack for Heritage Bread-Baking

1. Digital scale
2. Bowl scraper (white plastic)
3. Bench scraper (metal with wood handle)
4. Square plastic or other container with four edges (such as Cambro)
5. Large wood or stainless steel mixing bowl
6. 1-quart (1-L) plastic container with lid for starter
7. Fine-gauge cotton cheesecloth or linen napkin (not terry cloth, which sticks)
8. Two banneton baskets
9. Dutch oven or other ceramic or cast-iron pot with lid
10. Lame or utility knife for scoring
11. Pastry brush
12. Wooden cutting board for shaping
13. Electric stand mixer
14. Silicone baking mat (optional, for use in place of parchment paper or greasing)
15. Instant-read thermometer (optional, for serious accuracy when judging the temperature of water)
16. Baking stones (optional, for finishing one loaf while baking another in the same oven)

1
2
3
4
5
6
7
8
9
10
11
12
13
14
15
16

CHAPTER ONE

MASTER STARTER RECIPE

While we use instant yeast for enriched breads like brioche, nothing beats a true sourdough starter, which can be cultivated from naturally occurring yeast and bacteria in your home. There are many different terms that refer to a starter, such as *sourdough, mother, leaven,* or even the French *levain,* but all of these words mean the same thing: a treasured, living, breathing, and eating culture of healthy bacteria that helps break down the gluten. Natural starters bring out the nuanced flavors of heritage wheat and also add the touch of tang and sweetness that we crave in sourdough-style artisan bread.

LONG FERMENTATION IS KEY to authentic heritage baking. It takes a good amount of patience and time to develop a starter, which is why I recommend starting one on a lazy Sunday or another day that you're planning to stay close to home. Making a starter doesn't require a lot of hands-on technique, just a trusty scale and a good set of eyes with which to monitor its progress. Accuracy is key, so it's important to measure your starter ingredients in grams versus cups. While our recipes will still work if you're a little off on your flour or water amounts (by 15 g or so), it's best to measure as accurately as you can.

4 Tips for Starting Your Starter Successfully

1. Don't use antibacterial hand soap or cleaning products. Just a mild soap or even hot water on your hands is all you need when baking.
2. Use your hands! I know it might be uncomfortable, but if you are going to make bread, you need to get your hands dirty. Remove your rings and enjoy.
3. Use a clear container to hold the starter so that you can easily observe its activity.
4. Using freshly milled flour will work best because there is more enzymatic activity in recently milled flour.

THE HEWN HERITAGE STARTER

MAKES 400 G

At home, I like to create a starter that is as simple as possible. I prefer to use sifted heritage flour that has had some of the bran and germ removed. I don't get too hung up on how sifted it is, but we have had the best luck making a starter that is not 100 percent whole wheat (see Heritage Flour, Hewn Ingredients, and Equipment Primer, page 34). I also do not like using a flour that is so sifted that you can't see any of the germ or bran. You may find a local mill or farmer that has an all-purpose flour that will work well. My main point is don't get too focused on how sifted the flour is. If you can find a locally grown and stone-milled wheat that has about 10 to 20 percent of the bran and germ removed, that will create a great starter.

200 g lukewarm filtered water (77°F to 78°F [25°C to 25.5°C])

200 g sifted heritage flour or a heritage all-purpose flour

DAY 1

Start your starter. Place a 1-quart [960-ml] or larger clear container on a digital scale. Add the 200 g of lukewarm filtered water. You will add slightly warmer water now than during the regular feeding because the yeast loves to work in a 78°F [25.5°C] environment. Water quality can range from city to city, so I recommend using filtered water (see page 41).

Add the 200 g of heritage flour. Using your hands, mix the flour and water until the mixture is moistened and slightly sticky. There should not be any traces of flour; it should all

be mixed in. Cover the container loosely with cheesecloth or a linen napkin to let the starter breathe. Store the container on the kitchen counter away from sunlight at room temperature. During the colder winter months in the Midwest and East Coast, I put my starter near the furnace. For those who live in a warmer climate, this won't be necessary.

DAY 2

Check on your starter to see if there is any activity at all. You might see a bubble, or a hole where a bubble popped. If you don't see anything yet, don't panic! You can let your starter sit another day or up to 3 days until it's ready (we explain that later). Remember, patience is key. Let your starter sit another day before checking on it again.

DAY 3

100 g lukewarm filtered water

100 g sifted heritage flour or heritage AP flour

Inspect the starter. Do you see any bubbling? The starter might look like pancake batter, or it may just look liquidy and slimy on the top. It might even smell terrible, and that's OK. If nothing seems to be happening, or you're not seeing any bubbles at all, let your starter sit another day.

But if anything is happening—even if you just see a few little bubbles—get out your scale because it's time to take care of your pet starter. If you're not sure if "anything is happening," look along the sides and top of the container. If you see any holes or bubbles in the starter—no matter how small—it's time to feed it. If there is no activity, wait another day or two before inspecting again.

To feed your starter, set the container of 400 g of starter on a digital scale to weigh it. Then scoop out 200 g of the starter with your hands so you're left with 200 g still in the container. You can discard the scooped-out starter directly into the compost, or less ideally, your trash bin.

With the container of starter still on the scale, add 100 g of lukewarm filtered water (77°F to 78°F [25°C to 25.5°C]). Add 100 g of your flour mixture and mix with your hands until well combined and there are no visible traces of flour.

Re-cover you starter loosely with the cheesecloth or linen napkin.

DAYS 4 OR 5 THROUGH DAY 9

100 g lukewarm filtered water

100 g sifted heritage flour or heritage AP flour

Continue feeding your starter at roughly the same time every day. You will discard 200 g of starter, and then feed the remaining starter with 100 g of water and 100 g of the heritage flour or heritage AP flour and mix it together. Always re-cover the container with the cheesecloth or linen napkin.

By day 6 or 7, you should start to notice a more sour, slightly unpleasant smell. The starter will smell most sour just before feeding; after feeding, the alcoholic, sour smell dissipates because the starter is busy eating. Sometimes, just before feeding the starter, you might notice extra liquid collecting on the bottom of the

DAY 1
DAY 2
DAY 3
DAY 4

container. When the starter gets close to being ready, it will plump and open up with some bubbles and smell sweeter. The smell will remind you of a nice white vinegar.

To make sure your starter is continuing on the right path, check it about 3 hours after feeding. It should look pillowy and very bubbly and have risen by 1½ to 2 in [4 to 5 cm]. Once you start making bread, you will most likely use the starter 3 to 6 hours after feeding it, though it depends on the temperature of both the kitchen and the water. If you want to be very accurate, use a thermometer to take the temperature of the water before adding it to the starter. You will need to feed your starter for at least 10 days, possibly more, until it passes the Float Test (see right). Don't stress if it takes up to 2 weeks for your starter to finally be ready for baking.

DAY 10

200 g starter

100 g lukewarm filtered water

100 g sifted heritage flour or heritage AP flour

If all has gone well, the starter is now ready to be used for bread baking. To make bread on day 10, feed the starter a few hours before you want to mix the dough (feed the starter at 7 or 8 a.m. if you want to mix the dough at 11 a.m., or feed at 10 a.m. if you want to mix at 1 p.m., and so on).

Check on your starter about 3 hours after feeding. How do you truly know if your starter is ready? The starter should look like a hyper pancake batter. I describe it as bubbly, airy, and not too liquidy.

TIP

I recommend feeding the starter around the same time of day that you would most likely mix bread. You are training your starter to get on a schedule. I know it's crazy to think that yeast can be trained, but it can! Just like with a child or pet, being consistent and having a schedule is important when creating a starter. It will make your bread baking easier if your starter is fed at roughly the same time each day.

What if your starter still doesn't seem ready by day 10? Then I would recommend starting the process all over again. I know that sounds terribly time-consuming, but it's best to start with a clean state. Also remember that the more freshly milled your flour, the more activity there will be early on. If it means freshly milling your own flour, then that's the best method.

If your test worked and your starter is ready, congratulate yourself on creating a starter! Now you are closer to making naturally leavened, delicious, and healthy bread. Just remember to feed your starter as close to the same time of day as possible for 8 days.

Float Test

To be more accurate, try the Float Test. Fill a bowl with 4 in [10 cm] of room-temperature water. Take 1 tablespoon of the starter and place on top of the water. If it sinks to the bottom, the starter isn't ready. In that case, let your starter sit for another 30 to 45 minutes and test it again. If the starter floats like a little buoy, then it is ready to be used.

Maintaining Your Starter

If you're baking bread regularly—once a week or more—continue to feed the starter at about the same time every day. If taken care of properly, your starter can last a lifetime. More mature and beautiful flavors will develop over the years.

If you know you won't be baking bread again for a week or more, feed it once, and then put it in the refrigerator "to sleep." You can store the starter in the refrigerator for up to 2 weeks.

If You Go on Vacation

If you are going on vacation or know you won't make bread for a few weeks, feed your starter with flour and water like usual, and then refrigerate it for up to 4 weeks. When you come back, don't be concerned if it looks like a gray, sludgy, and oily mess. It will likely take 3 or 4 days of feeding it to get it ready to make bread again, but it will be just as good as before.

INSTRUCTIONS FOR FEEDING AFTER A VACATION

Day 1 / Dump all but 100 g of the sludgy, oily starter. Feed with 150 g filtered lukewarm water (76°F to 78°F [24.5°C to 25.5°C]) and 150 g of your flour mixture. Mix with your hands and let sit on your counter, covered with cheesecloth or a linen napkin, in its old, warm space.

Day 2 / Dump 200 g of the starter and repeat the feeding with 100 g water (76°F to 78°F [24°C to 25.5°C]) and 100 g of the heritage flour or heritage AP flour.

Day 3 / The starter should start looking like your old friend. Repeat the dumping and feeding process.

Day 4 / To make bread on day 4, feed your starter 3 to 4 hours before mixing the dough.

CHAPTER TWO

HERITAGE BREADS

HERITAGE BREAD MASTER FORMULA

MAKES 2 LOAVES

This is the basic how-to method for all of the heritage bread recipes in this book. The amount of flour, water, starter, and other ingredients will change from recipe to recipe. Start with the recipe for the bread you want to bake so you know how much you need for each ingredient, and then come back here for the step-by-step instructions.

VERY IMPORTANT: Heritage baking is a two-day process: After feeding the starter on the day you plan to bake, you will need to wait at least 3 hours, or up to overnight, until you can mix the dough. If you mix and shape the dough in the afternoon, you will likely need to wait until the next day to bake. Baking bread the heritage way takes extreme patience and is the ultimate test of delayed gratification, but trust me, it's worth it!

STEP 1

Feed the Starter for Bread Baking

PREP AND REST TIME 3 hours, up to overnight
EQUIPMENT NEEDED digital food scale, large mixing bowl

Feed the starter 3 to 4 hours before you plan to mix the dough. If your house is chilly (less than 60°F [16°C]), you may have to feed the starter the night before so it has enough time to ferment and has at least 8 hours to get to the point when it's ready. Again, you'll know it's ready if you test a bit of the starter in a bowl of lukewarm water and it floats to the top (see Float Test, page 51). After you feed the starter, it should be so bubbly and pillowy that you want to take a nap in it.

Put a large bowl on the scale and press "tare" to zero it out. Add your starter until the scale reads 200 g. Discard the rest of the starter or give it to a friend; don't worry, there will be more leftover starter when you're done baking.

Add 100 g of lukewarm (about 78°F [25.5°C]) water. Add 100 g of sifted white flour. The scale should read 400 g.

Mix with your hands until well combined. Cover loosely with cheesecloth or a linen napkin (not terry cloth, which can stick, shed lint, and/or suffocate the dough) and set in a warm place (ideal temperature is 76°F to 78°F [24°C to 25.5°C]) in the house or kitchen, such as near a stove.

After 3 hours, check your starter to see if it is ready. It should look airy with lots of bubbles.

Perform the Float Test (page 51) to see if it floats in a bowl of water. If it is not ready, let it sit for another 30 minutes in a warm location. Repeat the Float Test.

STEP 2

Mix and Autolyse

PREP AND RESTING TIME about 50 minutes
EQUIPMENT NEEDED food scale, large mixing bowl, bowl scraper

Autolyse refers to the stage after the starter, flour, and water are mixed, when it's allowed to rest, but before the salt. Think of it like a high school house party when the parents are out of town. It's the most fun time for the starter because there are no rules or restrictions, so it can just eat and bubble up and go crazy. Once the salt is added (or the parents come home), the party stops. Salt slows the yeast.

I like to mix my dough early in the morning, so I can bake in the afternoon or evening if my house is warm enough. It takes a while to fold the dough and let it ferment, so it's best to try to get started sooner than later. There's a reason people say we work baker's hours—we get things done early.

Once the starter passes the Float Test, put a large bowl on the scale and press "tare" to zero it out. Weigh out the amount of lukewarm water (about 78°F [25.5°C]) according to the bread recipe you've chosen. In a separate bowl, weigh out the additional water as called for in the recipe and set aside.

SAMPLE MORNING BAKING SCHEDULE

6 A.M. Feed the starter.

9 A.M. Mix the bread dough.

9:30 A.M. Add the salt.

9:30 A.M.–11:30 A.M. OR 12:30 P.M. Turn the dough.

11:30 P.M.–12:30 P.M. Divide the dough.

11:45 A.M. OR 12:45 P.M. Shape the dough, transfer to bannetons (baskets), and retard (rest) overnight in the refrigerator if baking the next day or set aside, covered, in a warmer spot (78°F/ 25.5°C is ideal) if baking the same day.

7 P.M. (OR LATER, BUT NO LATER THAN 10 A.M. THE NEXT DAY) Bake the bread.

SAMPLE AFTERNOON BAKING SCHEDULE

10:30 A.M. Feed the starter.

1:30 P.M. Mix the bread dough.

2 P.M. Add the salt.

2 P.M.–4 OR 5 P.M. Turn the dough.

4 P.M. OR 5 P.M. Divide the dough.

4:15 P.M. OR 5:15 P.M. Shape the dough, transfer to bannetons, and retard (rest) overnight in the refrigerator.

9 A.M. Bake the bread.

Tare the scale to zero again. Add the required amount of starter as called for in the recipe to the bowl with the water and stir gently with your hand until dissolved.

Tare the scale to zero again. Add the required amount of flour as called for in the recipe. Mix gently. Tare the scale again and add additional flour as needed, as specified by the recipe.

Using your hands and a bowl scraper, gently mix until all the flour is just a little wet. I take my bowl scraper and run it along the bottom and sides of the bowl while folding the dough over and onto itself with my free hand. This helps moisten any traces of dry flour.

If the dough appears shaggy and dry and there is still unmixed flour, add more water from your extra stash by dipping your hands in the water and continuing to mix. You don't want to pour the water in because the mixture may become too wet. The mixture should appear slightly sticky and tacky, but not runny and loose. Don't panic if the dough seems too dry—it will absorb water as it rests and you can always add a little more water later on if needed.

Cover the bowl with cheesecloth or a linen napkin (not terry cloth) and let rest for 40 minutes. If you leave the dough uncovered, it will dry out. It should be loosely covered.

Removing Flour from Your Hands the Sustainable Way

In my culinary school days, I spent time working on a sustainable farm in eastern Washington. At the time, there was a water shortage, so we could not use any unnecessary water. To remove flour from our hands when we made bread, we dredged them in a big bowl of dried flour and then rubbed our hands together. For rye breads, this is just about the only way to remove the slimy paste left behind on your hands; adding more water will just make your hands even slimier.

I was asked to demonstrate on a local Chicago channel how we mix and make bread. The host wanted to help mix, and I noticed her huge diamond ring just as her hands were going into the bowl to mix. Before I could say "stop!" her hands were coated as if she had just taken a concrete bath. As she mixed I joked that the dough was really coating her hands and ring, then she looked at me horrified and realized there was not going to be a way for her to get her hands cleaned before her next segment. When we went to commercial I pulled out a bowl of flour and had her rub her hands in it for a few minutes until she could at least see her fingers and ring again. So word to the wise . . . take off your rings, and don't do this on live TV!

STEP 3

Add Salt

PREP AND RESTING TIME about 40 minutes
EQUIPMENT NEEDED bowl scraper, 2-quart [2-L] square plastic container

As I mentioned earlier, the salt acts as the regulator or "buzzkill" for the party. Without salt, the starter would party all night and literally eat up all the sugars in the flour before having time to properly ferment. The salt slows the yeast down and allows the bread to ferment at a more consistent rate.

Working in two batches, sprinkle half of the salt called for in the recipe over the top of the dough. Moisten your hands by dipping them in your reserve water stash and slowly massage the dough until the salt granules have dissolved into the dough. Use a bowl scraper to fold the dough over two or three times. Add the remaining salt and use your hands to incorporate it into the dough. Imagine playing the piano and gently using your fingers to poke into the dough to dissolve the salt. You should not be able to see any salt granules; this shouldn't take more than a minute or two. Don't obsess too much about whether all of the salt has dissolved; you just don't want clumps of salt in the dough.

Transfer the dough from the bowl to a square plastic container (the square shape comes in handy when you fold the dough). Cover loosely with cheesecloth or a linen napkin and let sit for 30 minutes in a warmer part of the kitchen.

Water in Heritage Baking

Water is the main variable when working with heritage flours. Freshly milled flour tends to have more natural moisture content, so you won't need as much water when mixing. Wheat that was harvested in the fall and milled in the spring will be more dried out and might need more water. The amount of water you will need might even change with the season and your local weather. Rye bread in particular is one of the driest types of dough; it feels like concrete when you're mixing it. Rye also tends to absorb more water than wheat flours. Water in baking is like salt in cooking—once you add it, you can't take it back. It's best to start with less water rather than too much. That's why in all my bread recipes I call for an extra, separate reserve so I can add more water as needed by wetting my hand while mixing.

STEP 4

Fold

PREP AND RESTING TIME 2 to 3 hours
EQUIPMENT NEEDED 2-quart [2-L] square plastic container

This is the process of folding, or turning, the dough. The baking term is *bulk fermentation*. Many people think you have to knead bread in order to develop the gluten. Gently folding the dough takes the place of kneading. By folding the bread, you redistribute the ingredients and allow the starter to slowly digest the sugars and develop the gluten strands.

I think making bread this way is similar to sailing. It's all about adjusting your sails and using your skills to work gracefully with the wind rather than just sticking a key in the ignition of a speedboat and plowing through the water. So be gentle and try not to knead the dough, which can overwork the gluten in the flour and make the bread too tough and chewy. I prefer to use a square container when folding the dough because it's easier to turn the dough in a more concise, consistent manner. Note: Heritage Whole-Wheat Bread and Rye will go through 4 turns over the course of 2 hours. Heritage Country Bread and other breads using a blend of whole-wheat and sifted white flour will go through 6 turns over the course of 3 hours.

PUNCHING DOWN THE DOUGH

In other bread books, you might notice that a recipe calls for punching down the dough. At Hewn, we don't punch down the dough because we find that folding it (or turning it) is a more gentle way to redistribute the starter, salt, and other ingredients. And we actually want to keep some of the gas in the dough because it results in irregular holes. Because we use a natural starter and not an instant yeast one, there isn't an aggressive, quick rise and punching down is not necessary.

TURN 1 / Use your hands to dig down and reach the bottom of the dough. Gently lift and pull (don't tear) the dough and fold it over itself. Work each side like this until the dough has been lifted and folded 4 times. If adding extra ingredients such as cheese or herbs, add half of the amount specified in the recipe now. Let the dough sit, loosely covered with cheesecloth or a linen napkin (not terry cloth), for 30 minutes.

TURN 2 / Repeat the process for a second turn, adding the remaining extra ingredient, if using. Let sit, loosely covered, for 30 minutes.

TURNS 3 TO 6 / Repeat the process for the third through sixth turns, depending on how many turns the recipe specifies. Let the dough sit, loosely covered, for 30 minutes after each turn.

TIP

We're all busy people and it's really easy to lose count of your turns. The best way to keep track is to write out the turn schedule and cross off each time you complete the turn. I often write these notes on a piece of tape attached to the top of the container, but you can use a separate piece of paper, sticky note, or whatever works for you. Accidentally skipping a turn or letting the dough sit too long could lead to a flatter bread because the yeast will not be redistributed as evenly. You don't want 4 hours to go by without giving the dough a single turn. If you do happen to forget just 1 turn, though, don't despair. Just continue on with the other turns until you complete 4 (or 6) total, depending on which bread you're making.

STEP 5

Divide

PREP TIME 5 to 15 minutes
EQUIPMENT NEEDED metal bench scraper

This is the process of cutting the dough in half to prepare two dough balls for shaping and baking.

Transfer the dough to a wooden cutting board or smooth counter. Wood is best because it allows the bread to lightly stick to it. A granite, marble, or steel surface can get too slippery. This can make it more difficult to create surface tension on the exterior of the dough, which you need so the bread can bake with a beautiful crust. If you don't have a wooden cutting board, even a sanded piece of untreated wood will work.

Using your bench scraper, cut the dough in half using one clean cut. Using your scale, make sure the pieces are about the same weight, no more than 30 g off. If you need to adjust the pieces, use your bench scraper to cut and add more dough to the lighter half. With your hands, gently shape each piece of dough into a ball, but don't try to make them too perfect. Restrain yourself from working the dough too much as you shape the balls. Let the balls sit for 15 minutes to rest. If you work the dough too much and don't let it rest, it won't stretch as easily, which will make it harder to get a nice, tight skin.

TIP

A metal bench scraper is important for dividing bread dough because you want a clean cut. You can also use a sharp chef's knife.

STEP 6

Shape

PREP TIME about 10 minutes
EQUIPMENT NEEDED 2 banneton baskets

There are many ways to shape bread, but to simplify our lives, we will be using one shape for all the breads in this book: a bâtard, or oval "football" shape. Describing how to shape bread is like trying to describe how to change a cloth diaper on a newborn. When you watch someone do it a few times, it's easy, but to learn through a book takes a little more focus until you can just jump in and start practicing. At least shaping bread is a more pleasant experience than changing a diaper!

Working with one ball at a time, using your right hand, stretch the right side of the dough ball outward about 6 in [15 cm] and fold it back over onto itself toward the middle point of the dough ball. Repeat the process using your left hand on the left side. Next, take the top part of the dough ball and stretch it out about 6 in [15 cm] and fold that piece over the other folds—this is the seam side.

Flip the seam side down, so the seams are touching the cutting board or table. You can use your bench scraper to push the dough to seal the seam on the bottom and create a really tight skin on the top. You want to have a nice tight dough ball. If you see little gas bubbles, that is great work! Don't pop those bubbles; let the skin stay tight and keep all that gas contained. It will help the bread form a tight crust and open up nicely when the bread is baked. When you see a great piece of chewy, sourdough-like bread with all the little holes in the middle, that's from those gas bubbles.

Lightly dust the inside of your banneton baskets with flour so the dough doesn't stick to them. Working with one dough ball at a time, slide the bench scraper underneath the dough and flip it into the banneton so that the seam side is up.

TIP

The master formula calls for making two loaves instead of one because it's easier to work with a larger volume of dough. Anyone who bakes bread naturally makes more friends because there's always a freshly baked loaf to give away!

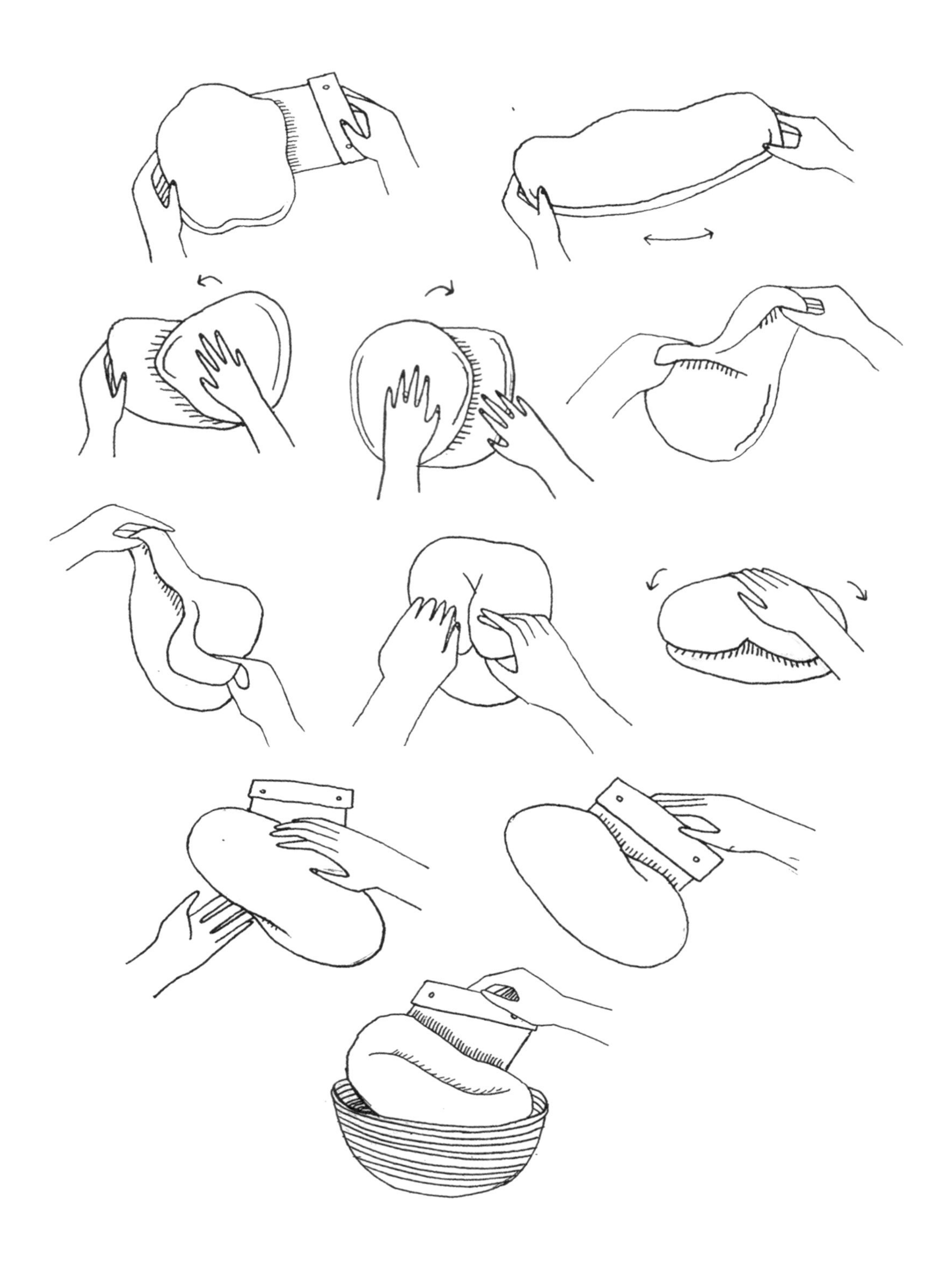

STEP 7

Sleep

RESTING TIME 6 hours to overnight

Retarding the dough means that you're letting the dough sleep for a bit. This is different than conventional bread baking. The dough rests at a refrigerated or room temperature rather than at higher temperatures, which would cause the dough to over-ferment and create a flat loaf. As a result, it takes longer to bake this way, but it is still possible to bake the same day if your room temperature is a little higher (ideally 78°F to 80°F [25°C to 26°C]).

TO BAKE THE SAME DAY / If you started mixing your dough early in the day and plan to bake later that afternoon or evening, let the dough rest in the bannetons, each loosely covered with cheesecloth or a linen napkin, in a warm place in the kitchen for 6 to 8 hours, or until the bread has filled the basket. It may sound extreme, but if you plan to bake the same day, measure how much space is between the dough and the top of the basket. Ideally you would want to bake the bread once the dough has risen to within ½ in [12 mm] of the basket. If you bake too soon, before the dough has properly risen, the loaf will turn out flat.

TO BAKE THE NEXT DAY / Place the covered bannetons in the refrigerator. Retarding the dough in the refrigerator slows down the yeast and allows for a long, slow fermentation. The longer the dough retards, the more acidic and complex its flavor becomes—similar to sourdough bread. If you don't have time to bake the bread the next day, don't fret! Just bake it early the day after that—preferably before 10 a.m. When ready to bake, remove the dough from the refrigerator and let it come to room temperature. This is usually about the same amount of time it takes to preheat the oven.

STEP 8

Bake

BAKING TIME 28 minutes
EQUIPMENT NEEDED large cast-iron Dutch oven, cheesecloth or linen napkin, lame or utility knife razor, flat metal spatula

Place a large round or oval ceramic Dutch oven or cast-iron pot, with its cover on, on the middle rack of the oven. Preheat the oven to 475°F [240°C]. When the oven reaches temperature, remove the pot from the oven and set it on the top of your stove. Remove the lid and set it aside. While baking the first loaf, leave the other in the refrigerator until the first loaf is baked. Then repeat the baking steps to bake the second loaf.

To transfer the dough to the pot, loosen the edges of the dough in the banneton gently with your hands. Place cheesecloth or a linen napkin over the pot rim on the side closest to your working hand; this will keep you from burning yourself. Rest the back of your hand along the cloth-covered rim to steady yourself, and quickly overturn the dough from the basket, flipping it into the middle of the pot.

If the dough lands partially on the side of the pot, it is better to keep it there than try to move it. Consider it as you would a failed free throw attempt in basketball, and just try to do better next time. The bread will still taste great, but it just might be a little misshapen.

To score the bread, hold your lame or utility knife at a 30-degree angle. With confidence, quickly make two ¼-in- [6-mm-] deep diagonal slashes along the top of the bread. The slashes should be approximately 2 in [5 cm] long.

Cover the pot and bake for 14 minutes, until the dough is still light blonde in color, but evenly baked and firm on the bottom. Remove from the oven, remove the lid, and using a flat metal spatula, gently loosen the bottom of the bread so it's not sticking to the pot.

Why do we score bread?

Cutting into the dough releases some of the pressure and steam, so that the bread doesn't crack and blow out. If the dough doesn't have a way for the steam to escape, it will explode out the sides and look really nasty. But if you slash the top of the loaf, the dough rises up nicely and evenly during baking.

Return the Dutch oven to the oven and bake, uncovered, for another 14 minutes, until the bread is a deep amber color, with a golden crust. Using your spatula, transfer the bread to a wooden cutting board, wire rack, or butcher's block to cool.

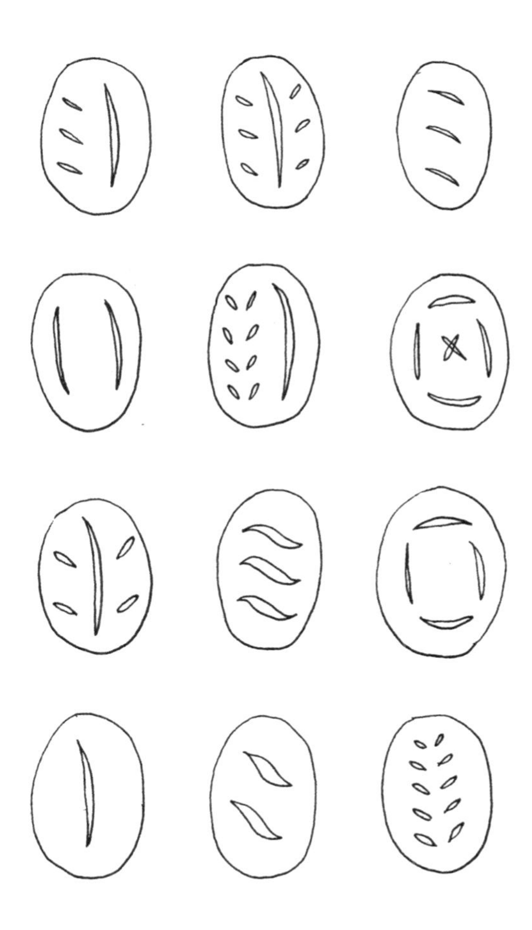

Serve and Store

COOLING TIME 20 minutes
EQUIPMENT NEEDED serrated knife, resealable plastic bag or container

Nothing beats freshly baked bread, straight from the oven. But the good news is, heritage breads actually freeze really well, so you can enjoy them beyond the first few days.

Let the bread rest for 30 minutes before slicing and serving with your favorite butter or olive oil, or for using in sandwiches.

To store for short-term use, keep in an airtight bread box. You can also leave it cut-side down on your counter or cutting board. Personally, I like to wrap it in beeswax paper, an all-natural storage wrap. Not only does the beeswax paper help the bread stay soft and moist for up to 5 days, but it's also reusable and can be used for up to a year.

To store for long-term use, let cool completely before slicing. Freeze in a resealable plastic bag or container for up to 2 months. When ready to use, thaw on the countertop for about an hour and refresh in the oven at 350°F [175°C] for 5 to 10 minutes. Some people like to slice the bread first prior to freezing it, which makes it easy to pull out a slice and put it directly into the toaster.

The Bread Equation

Baking is all about math and formulas. It can be intimidating. However, take heart in knowing that baker's math is not as challenging as, say, calculus. Bread is all about percentages and weights, which is why we use scales instead of cups and spoons to measure the ingredients.

We use a single equation to calculate all of the formulas for breads, no matter what the type. Essentially, the total weight of the flour determines the amount of water, salt, and any additional ingredients. Here is an example of an equation we use:

Ingredient Weight = Ingredient Percent x Total Flour Weight

So, if I use **1,000 g** of flour, I would multiply that by **80 percent**, which leaves me with **800 g** of water. If I want to add **18 percent** starter, per a specific bread recipe, I would take **1,000 g** of flour and multiply that by **18 percent** to get **180 g** of starter.

Don't worry; I have completed all of the math for you in this book because I want you to be able to bake bread, stress-free, at home. Still, it's always good to at least have a basic understanding of the foundations of heritage bread baking.

HERITAGE COUNTRY

MAKES 2 LOAVES

135 g starter (page 47)

500 g water, plus 30 g as needed (76°F to 78°F [24.5°C to 25.5°C])

510 g sifted heritage flour (HRW/HRS), such as Red Fife

200 g heritage whole-wheat flour (HRW/HRS), such as Rouge de Bordeaux

14 g fine sea salt

My nickname for this loaf is urban bread because it's the base for many of the breads we make at the bakery, except our Heritage Whole-Wheat bread (page 76). A rustic, jack-of-all-trades loaf, it's delicious simply slathered with butter or used for your favorite sandwich. This is also the best bread to start with when learning how to bake bread. At Hewn, we test out new varieties of wheat flour using this formula because it's a pretty forgiving recipe. We prefer using Rouge de Bordeaux, Red Fife, or the Pfeiffer heritage wheat varieties because of the tangy, sourdough-like flavor.

Feed and rest your starter (see Step 1 of the Master Formula, page 54).

Once the starter is ready, set a large bowl on the scale. Weigh out 500 g of water. Measure the 30 g of reserve water and set aside.

Return the bowl of water to the scale and tare the scale to zero. Add the starter and, using your hand, dissolve it gently in the water.

Tare the scale to zero again. Add the sifted and whole-wheat flours. Using your hands and a bowl scraper, gently mix until all the flour is just a little wet (see Step 2 of the Master Formula, page 55). If the dough is shaggy and dry, add more water from your extra stash by dipping your hands in the water and continuing to mix until it is slightly sticky.

Cover with cheesecloth or a linen napkin and let rest for 40 minutes.

Continued . . .

Working in batches, sprinkle 5 g of the salt over the top of the dough (see Step 3 of the Master Formula, page 58). Moisten hands by dipping them in your reserve water stash and slowly massage the dough until the salt granules have dissolved into the mixture. Use a bowl scraper to fold the dough over and onto itself. Add 5 g more of the salt, mixing until dissolved. Add the remaining 4 g salt and mix until dissolved completely, dipping your hands in the water as needed.

Transfer the dough from the bowl to a shallow square plastic container, cover loosely with cheesecloth or a linen napkin, and let sit for 30 minutes in a warm place.

Use your hands to dig down and reach the bottom of the dough (see Step 4 of the Master Formula, page 59). Gently lift and pull (don't tear) the dough and fold it over itself. Work each side like this until the dough has been lifted and folded 4 times. Let sit, loosely covered, for 30 minutes. Repeat the process for a second, third, fourth, and fifth turn and let sit, covered, for 30 minutes after each turn. Perform the sixth turn and let sit, covered, for 30 minutes.

Divide (or bake as Pan Bread, see page 79), shape, sleep, and bake the dough as instructed in Steps 5 through 8 of the Heritage Bread Master Formula (pages 61 through 65). See Step 9 for serving and storage (page 68).

CHEDDAR COUNTRY BREAD

MAKES 2 LOAVES

135 g starter (page 47)

500 g water, plus 30 g as needed (76°F to 78°F [24.5°C to 25.5°C]),

510 g sifted heritage wheat flour (HRW/HRS), such as Glenn

200 g heritage whole-wheat flour (HRW/HRS), such as Rouge de Bordeaux or Turkey Red

14 g fine sea salt

200 g shredded white cheddar cheese

This bread is one of my favorites. I like to use a sharp white cheddar for a richer, cheesier taste. If the cheddar is too mild, the flavor won't come through in the baked bread. Hands down, this is the best bread for making grilled cheese; as the bread toasts, the infused cheddar caramelizes, creating addictive, crispy pieces. Use a box grater to shred the cheese, or for a faster method, you can break it up into tiny bits in a food processor with the regular blade attachment.

Feed and rest your starter (see Step 1 of the Master Formula, page 54).

Once the starter is ready, set a large bowl on the scale. Weigh out 500 g of water. Measure the 30 g reserve water and set aside.

Return the bowl of water to the scale and tare the scale to zero. Add the starter and, using your hand, dissolve it gently in the water.

Tare the scale to zero again. Add the sifted and whole-wheat flours. Using your hands and a bowl scraper, gently mix until all the flour is just a little wet (see Step 2 of the Master Formula, page 55). If the dough is shaggy and dry, add more water from your extra stash by dipping your hands in the water and continuing to mix until it is slightly sticky.

Cover with cheesecloth or a linen napkin and let rest for 40 minutes.

Working in batches, sprinkle 5 g of the salt over the top of the dough (see Step 3 of the Master Formula, page 58). Moisten hands by dipping them in your reserve water stash and slowly

Continued . . .

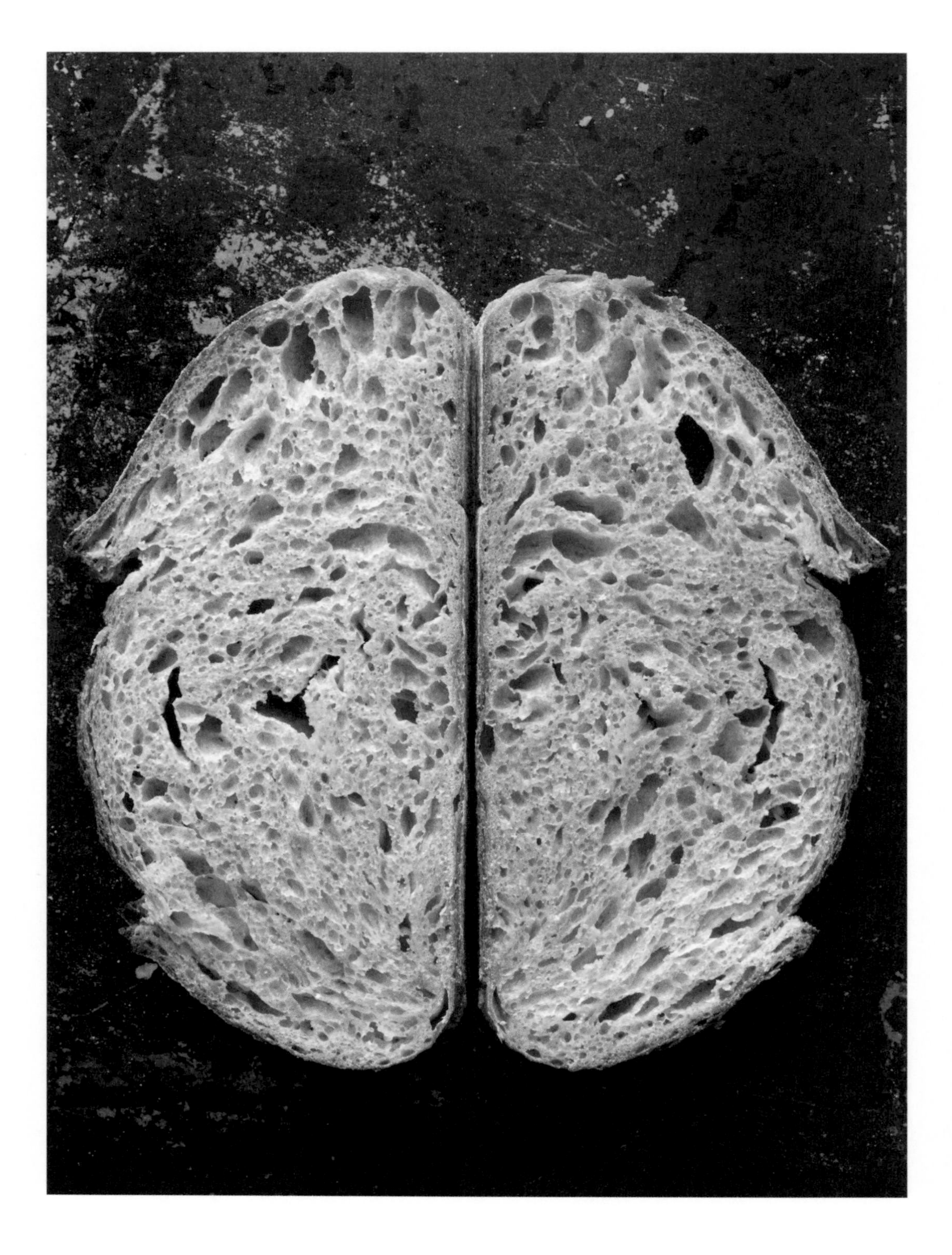

massage the dough until the salt granules have dissolved into the mixture. Use a bowl scraper to fold the dough over and onto itself. Add 5 g more of the salt, mixing until dissolved. Add the remaining 4 g salt and mix until dissolved completely, dipping your hands in the water as needed.

Transfer the dough from the bowl to a shallow square plastic container, cover loosely with cheesecloth or a linen napkin, and let sit for 30 minutes in a warm place.

Use your hands to dig down and reach the bottom of the dough (see Step 4 of the Master Formula, page 59). Gently lift and pull (don't tear) the dough and fold it over itself. Work each side like this until the dough has been lifted and folded 4 times. Let sit, loosely covered, for 30 minutes. Repeat the process for a second turn, but add 50 g of the cheese on top of the dough, and fold one side of the dough over the cheese. Add another 50 g, and fold the dough over the cheese. Repeat 2 more times until all the cheese is added. Let sit, covered, for 30 minutes. Repeat the process for a third, fourth, and fifth turn and let sit, covered, for 30 minutes after each turn. Perform the sixth turn and let sit, covered, for 30 minutes.

Divide (or bake as Pan Bread, see page 79), shape, sleep, and bake the dough as instructed in Steps 5 through 8 of the Heritage Bread Master Formula (pages 61 through 65). See step 9 for serving and storage (page 68).

HERITAGE WHOLE WHEAT

MAKES 2 LOAVES

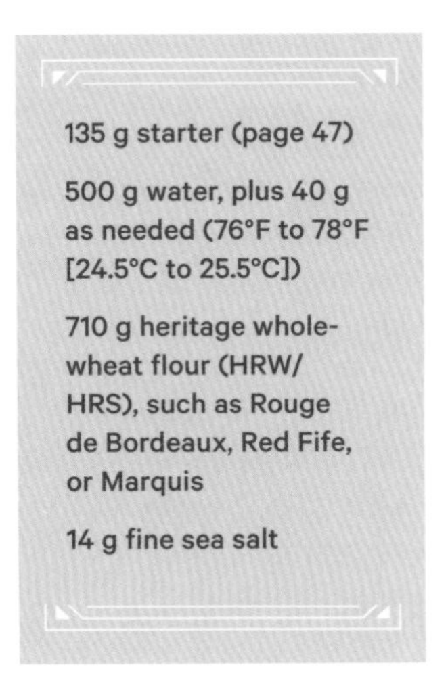

135 g starter (page 47)

500 g water, plus 40 g as needed (76°F to 78°F [24.5°C to 25.5°C])

710 g heritage whole-wheat flour (HRW/HRS), such as Rouge de Bordeaux, Red Fife, or Marquis

14 g fine sea salt

At Hewn, we use a variety of heritage whole-wheat flours (see Heritage Flour, Hewn Ingredient, and Equipment Primer, page 34). The intensity of the wheat flavor will vary depending on which type you use, but overall, this bread has a rich and nutty crumb that pairs incredibly well with raspberry jam or a dollop of chive-infused goat cheese. You can also go all out and try it with gravlax and crème fraîche.

Feed and rest your starter (see Step 1 of the Master Formula, page 54).

Once the starter is ready, set a large bowl on the scale. Weigh out 500 g of water. Measure the 40 g reserve water and set aside.

Return the bowl of water to the scale and tare the scale to zero. Add the starter and, using your hand, dissolve it gently in the water.

Tare the scale to zero again. Add the whole-wheat flour. Using your hands and a bowl scraper, gently mix until all the flour is just a little wet (see Step 2 of the Master Formula, page 55). If the dough is shaggy and dry, add more water from your extra stash by dipping your hands in the water and continuing to mix until it is slightly sticky.

Cover with cheesecloth or a linen napkin and let rest for 40 minutes.

Working in batches, sprinkle 5 g of salt over the top of the dough (see Step 3 of the Master Formula, page 58). Moisten hands by dipping them in your reserve water stash and slowly massage the dough until the salt granules have dissolved into

Continued . . .

the mixture. Use a bowl scraper to fold the dough over and onto itself. Add 5 g of salt, mixing until dissolved. Add the remaining 4 g salt and mix until dissolved completely, dipping your hands in the water as needed.

Transfer the dough from the bowl to a shallow square plastic container, cover loosely with cheesecloth or a linen napkin, and let sit for 30 minutes in a warm place.

Use your hands to dig down and reach the bottom of the dough (see Step 4 of the Master Formula, page 59). Gently lift and pull (don't tear) the dough and fold it over itself. Work each side like this until the dough has been lifted and folded 4 times. Let sit, loosely covered, for 30 minutes. Repeat the process for a second turn and let sit, covered, for 30 minutes, then perform the third turn and let sit, covered, for 30 minutes.

Divide (or bake as Pan Bread, see page 79), shape, sleep, and bake the dough as instructed in Steps 5 through 8 of the Heritage Bread Master Formula (pages 61 through 65). See Step 9 for serving and storage (page 68).

PAN BREAD

MAKES 1 LOAF

1 kg dry Heritage Bread dough

Want bread for sandwiches? Don't have a banneton yet? You can take any of the bread recipes in this chapter and bake the dough in a greased 8-by-4-in [20-by-10-cm] loaf pan if you want sliced bread for sandwiches. I like to use this method to make sandwich slices out of the Heritage Country, Heritage Whole-Wheat, and Seeded Whole-Wheat breads, but you can use the pan bread method for any of the bread recipes in this chapter.

Follow the Heritage Bread Master Formula (page 54), completing Steps 1 through 4. Instead of dividing the dough in half in step 5, weigh out 1 kg of the dough.

Wrap and store the remaining dough in the refrigerator and use within the following 24 hours for the Heritage Flatbread recipe (page 113), or bake using a mini loaf pan if you have one.

Working with the 1 kg of dough, shape the dough following Step 6 of the Heritage Bread Master Formula (page 62). Instead of placing the shaped dough in a banneton, place it seam-side down in an 8-by-4-inch [20-by-10-cm] loaf pan lightly sprayed with olive oil.

Allow the bread to sit in the pan, covered loosely with cheesecloth or a linen napkin, overnight in a warm place in the kitchen to rise. There is no need to score this bread, but you can top a whole-wheat version lightly with stone-rolled oats just before baking in the oven.

Approximately 30 minutes before baking, preheat the oven to 475°F [240°C].

Continued . . .

Tent the bread pan with aluminum foil, wrapping the edges with foil but allowing for headroom to give the dough room to rise.

Bake for 15 minutes. Remove the foil, and carefully rotate the pan and bake for another 15 minutes or until just browned on top.

Remove the bread from the pan to cool: Wearing oven mitts, hold the pan with one hand and flip over the pan, catching the bread in the palm of your other, mitt-covered hand. Cool on a wire rack for 30 minutes before slicing and serving warm or using for sandwiches. See Step 9 of the Heritage Bread Master Formula (page 68) for long-term storage.

MIDWEST BLEND

MAKES 2 LOAVES

- 135 g starter (page 47)
- 530 g water, plus 40 g as needed (76°F to 78°F [24.5°C to 25.5°C])
- 350 g heritage whole-wheat or sifted heritage flour (HRW/HRS), such as Turkey Red or Marquis
- 250 g spelt flour
- 110 g sifted heritage flour (HRW/HRS), such as Red Fife
- 14 g fine sea salt

I like to think of this bread as the showcase for the best heritage whole-wheat flours I can find. It is a great base for experimenting; while I use many midwestern heritage whole-wheat flours, you might want to experiment with the local flours from your area. Just stick with hard red winter or spring flours (a mixture of 100 percent whole wheat and sifted flours, or all sifted) for a total flour amount of 710 g. It's also important to have a little extra water on hand when mixing. When experimenting with flour varieties from around the country, you won't know how much natural moisture they contain. If the dough feels dry after the salt is added, dunk your hands in your reserve water stash and turn the dough a couple more times to moisten.

Feed and rest your starter (see Step 1 of the Master Formula, page 54).

Once the starter is ready, set a large bowl on the scale. Weigh out 530 g of water. Measure the 40 g of reserve water and set aside.

Return the bowl of water to the scale and tare the scale to zero. Add the starter and, using your hand, dissolve it gently in the water.

Tare the scale to zero again. Add the whole-wheat, spelt, and sifted flours. Using your hands and a bowl scraper, gently mix until all the flour is just a little wet (see Step 2 of the Master Formula, page 55). If the dough is shaggy and dry, add more water from your extra stash by dipping your hands in the water and continuing to mix until it is slightly sticky.

Continued . . .

Cover with cheesecloth or a linen napkin and let rest for 40 minutes.

Working in batches, sprinkle 5 g of the salt over the top of the dough (see Step 3 of the Master Formula, page 58). Moisten hands by dipping them in your reserve water stash and slowly massage the dough until the salt granules have dissolved into the mixture. Use a bowl scraper to fold the dough over and onto itself. Add 5 g more of the salt, mixing until dissolved. Add the remaining 4 g salt and mix until dissolved completely, dipping your hands in the water as needed.

Transfer the dough from the bowl to a shallow square plastic container, cover loosely with cheesecloth or a linen napkin, and let sit for 30 minutes in a warm place.

Use your hands to dig down and reach the bottom of the dough (see Step 4 of the Master Formula, page 59). Gently lift and pull (don't tear) the dough and fold it over itself. Work each side like this until the dough has been lifted and folded 4 times. Let sit, loosely covered, for 30 minutes. Repeat the process for a second turn and let sit, covered, for 30 minutes, then perform the third turn and let sit, covered, for 30 minutes.

Divide (or bake as Pan Bread, see page 79), shape, sleep, and bake the dough as instructed in Steps 5 through 8 of the Heritage Bread Master Formula (pages 61 through 65). See Step 9 (page 68) for serving and storage.

SEEDED WHOLE WHEAT

MAKES 2 LOAVES

- 135 g starter (page 47)
- 530 g water, plus 25 g as needed (76°F to 78°F [24.5°C to 25.5°C])
- 560 g heritage whole-wheat flour (HRW/HRS), such as Glenn or Rouge de Bordeaux
- 150 g sifted heritage flour (HRW/HRS), such as Turkey Red
- 5 g flaxseeds
- 5 g millet seeds
- 25 g sunflower seeds, toasted
- 25 g pumpkin seeds, toasted
- 5 g chia seeds
- 14 g fine sea salt

This is a Hewn Bakery favorite. We pack the bread with as many seeds as we think it can handle. Adding a bit of sifted heritage flour helps bind the dough with a little extra strength because all the seeds can weigh the bread down. Feel free to omit a seed but add more of another type to keep the recipe balanced. You can also top the loaf with more seeds before baking. Just watch the seeds on the top when the lid is removed so they don't burn. You might need to reduce the final baking time by a few minutes as a result.

Feed and rest your starter (see Step 1 of the Master Formula, page 54).

Once the starter is ready, set a large bowl on the scale. Weigh out 500 g of water. Measure the 25 g of reserve water and set aside.

Return the bowl of water to the scale and tare the scale to zero. Add the starter and, using your hand, dissolve it gently in the water.

Tare the scale to zero again. Add the whole-wheat and sifted flours. Using your hands and a bowl scraper, gently mix until all the flour is just a little wet (see Step 2 of the Master Formula, page 55). If the dough is shaggy and dry, add more water from your extra stash by dipping your hands in the water and continuing to mix until it is slightly sticky.

Cover with cheesecloth or a linen napkin and let rest for 40 minutes.

Continued . . .

Prepare the flaxseeds and millet seeds. Pour 20 g of boiling water over the flax and millet. Cover with foil and let cool. Drain. Mix with the sunflower, pumpkin, and chia seeds.

Working in batches, sprinkle 5 g of the salt over the top of the dough (see Step 3 of the Master Formula, page 58). Moisten hands by dipping them in your reserve water stash and slowly massage the dough until the salt granules have dissolved into the mixture. Use a bowl scraper to fold the dough over and onto itself. Add 5 g more of the salt, mixing until dissolved. Add the remaining 4 g salt and mix until dissolved completely, dipping your hands in the water as needed.

Transfer the dough from the bowl to a shallow square plastic container, cover loosely with cheesecloth or a linen napkin, and let sit for 30 minutes in a warm place.

Use your hands to dig down and reach the bottom of the dough (see Step 4 of the Master Formula, page 59). Gently lift and pull (don't tear) the dough and fold it over itself. Work each side like this until the dough has been lifted and folded 4 times. On the second fold, spread the seed mixture over the dough and continue with the folds. Let sit, loosely covered, for 30 minutes. Repeat the process for a second turn and let sit, covered, for 30 minutes, then perform the third turn and let sit, covered, for 30 minutes.

Divide (or bake as Pan Bread, see page 79), shape, sleep, and bake the dough as instructed in Steps 5 through 8 of the Heritage Bread Master Formula (pages 61 through 65). See Step 9 for serving and storage (page 68).

TURKEY RED AND GRUYÈRE

MAKES 2 LOAVES

135 g starter (page 47)

530 g water, plus 25 g as needed (76°F to 78°F [24.5°C to 25.5°C])

610 g heritage whole-wheat flour (HRW/HRS), such as Turkey Red

100 g sifted heritage flour (HRW/HRS)

14 g fine sea salt

200 g cave-aged Gruyère cheese, shredded

Turkey Red is a wheat variety brought to Kansas by Mennonite farmers fleeing religious persecution in Russia in the late 1870s. This hard red winter wheat was one of the primary varieties of wheat grown for seventy years in the Midwest. It grew incredibly well in Kansas and it was planted in more than 75 percent of the fields in the early twentieth century. After World War II, when industrial farming started taking hold, this variety faded away. Conventional varieties with mythically high yields that were dependent on synthetic inputs (herbicides, pesticides, and so on) were planted instead of the flavorful heritage varieties, such as this one. Turkey Red is making a comeback, however, in Kansas, Wisconsin, and other parts of the Midwest. It has a robust, earthy taste and hearty texture, but it's not overbearing. I like to add a little sifted flour to create a lighter, more balanced loaf, but you could use 100 percent Turkey Red. The buttery richness of the Gruyère just helps smooth everything out.

FUN FACT: There is actually a museum devoted to the Mennonite farmers who brought over Turkey Red seeds from Russia in 1874. If you're ever in the Kansas City area, head to the small town of Goessel and tour the Mennonite Heritage and Agricultural Museum to see the Turkey Red Wheat Palace.

Feed and rest your starter (see Step 1 of the Master Formula, page 54).

Once the starter is ready, set a large bowl on the scale. Weigh out 530 g of water. Measure the 25 g of reserved water and set aside.

Continued . . .

Return the bowl of water to the scale and tare the scale to zero. Add the starter and, using your hand, dissolve it gently in the water.

Tare the scale to zero again. Add the whole-wheat and sifted flours. Using your hands and a bowl scraper, gently mix until all the flour is just a little wet (see Step 2 of the Master Formula, page 55). If the dough is shaggy and dry, add more water from your extra stash by dipping your hands in the water and continuing to mix until it is slightly sticky.

Cover with cheesecloth or a linen napkin and let rest for 40 minutes.

Working in batches, sprinkle 5 g of the salt over the top of the dough (see Step 3 of the Master Formula, page 58). Moisten hands by dipping them in your reserve water stash and slowly massage the dough until the salt granules have dissolved into the mixture. Use a bowl scraper to fold the dough over and onto itself. Add 5 g more of the salt, mixing until dissolved. Add the remaining 4 g salt and mix until dissolved completely, dipping your hands in the water as needed.

Transfer the dough from the bowl to a shallow square plastic container, cover loosely with cheesecloth or a linen napkin, and let sit for 30 minutes in a warm place.

Use your hands to dig down and reach the bottom of the dough (see Step 4 of the Master Formula, page 59). Gently lift and pull (don't tear) the dough and fold it over itself. Work each side like this until the dough has been lifted and folded 4 times. Let sit, loosely covered, for 30 minutes. Repeat the process for a second turn and add the cheese by sprinkling it on top of the dough as you fold it. Let sit, covered, for 30 minutes, then perform the third turn and let sit, covered, for 30 minutes.

Divide (or bake as Pan Bread, see page 79), shape, sleep, and bake the dough as instructed in Steps 5 through 8 of the Heritage Bread Master Formula (pages 61 through 65). See Step 9 for serving and storage (page 68).

HERITAGE SPELT

2 LOAVES

130 g starter (page 47)

525 g water, plus 25 g as needed (76°F to 78°F [24.5°C to 25.5°C])

640 g spelt flour

70 g sifted heritage flour (HRW/HRS), such as Turkey Red

14 g fine sea salt

So what is spelt anyway? Is it an ancient grain? Not really. Spelt is like the odd cousin or distant relative that's not quite like the rest of a family. Spelt has a different gluten structure than wheat. It still has gluten, but less of it, and that's why some people say they tolerate spelt bread better than higher-gluten, whole-wheat breads. Bread made with spelt has a really deep, earthy taste and heartiness, such that I can only eat one or two slices before feeling full. I love it! We source our spelt from two great farms: Meadowlark Organics (see page 168) in Wisconsin's Driftless Region and Meuer Farm, outside of Green Bay. There are actually different varieties of spelt; we work with the Sun Gold and Maverick varieties. This formula uses 90 percent spelt and 10 percent sifted heritage flour to lighten it up, but feel free to use 100 percent spelt if you want to pack a bigger flavor punch.

Feed and rest your starter (see Step 1 of the Master Formula, page 54).

Once the starter is ready, set a large bowl on the scale. Weigh out 525 g of water. Measure the reserve 25 g of water and set aside.

Return the bowl of water to the scale and tare the scale to zero. Add the starter and, using your hand, dissolve it gently in the water.

Continued . . .

Tare the scale to zero again. Add the spelt and sifted flours. Using your hands and a bowl scraper, gently mix until all the flour is just a little wet (see Step 2 of the Master Formula, page 55). If the dough is shaggy and dry, add more water from your extra stash by dipping your hands in the water and continuing to mix until it is slightly sticky.

Cover with cheesecloth or a linen napkin and let rest for 40 minutes.

Working in batches, sprinkle 5 g of the salt over the top of the dough (see Step 3 of the Master Formula, page 58). Moisten hands by dipping them in your reserve water stash and slowly massage the dough until the salt granules have dissolved into the mixture. Use a bowl scraper to fold the dough over and onto itself. Add 5 g more of the salt, mixing until dissolved. Add the remaining 4 g salt and mix until dissolved completely, dipping your hands in the water as needed.

Transfer the dough from the bowl to a shallow square plastic container, cover loosely with cheesecloth or a linen napkin, and let sit for 30 minutes in a warm place.

Use your hands to dig down and reach the bottom of the dough (see Step 4 of the Master Formula, page 59). Gently lift and pull (don't tear) the dough and fold it over itself. Work each side like this until the dough has been lifted and folded 4 times. Let sit, loosely covered, for 30 minutes. Repeat the process for a second turn and let sit, covered, for 30 minutes, then perform the third turn and let sit, covered, for 30 minutes.

Divide (or bake as Pan Bread, see page 79), shape, sleep, and bake the dough as instructed in Steps 5 through 8 of the Heritage Bread Master Formula (pages 61 through 65). See Step 9 for serving and storage (page 68).

PARMESAN GARLIC

MAKES 2 LOAVES

135 g starter (page 47)

500 g water, plus 30 g as needed (76°F to 78°F [24.5°C to 25.5°C])

510 g sifted heritage flour (HRW/HRS), such as Turkey Red or Glenn

200 g heritage whole-wheat flour (HRW/HRS), such as Red Fife

14 g fine sea salt

175 g grated Parmesan cheese

10 g minced garlic

This bread is the best replacement for any old garlic bread. You can use raw garlic for a stronger flavor, or roasted garlic for a milder, nutty flavor (see Note, page 96). I like to use a Parmesan cheese that's been aged for at least 12 months. The longer a cheese has been aged, the more protein crystals are present, which create a stronger flavor without all the moisture that comes from a fresher cheese. Too much moisture can throw off a bread recipe, especially when working with heritage flours, which already have greater moisture content.

Feed and rest your starter (see Step 1 of the Master Formula, page 54).

Once the starter is ready, set a large bowl on the scale. Weigh out 500 g of water. Measure the 30 g of reserve water and set aside.

Return the bowl of water to the scale and tare the scale to zero. Add the starter and, using your hand, dissolve it gently in the water.

Tare the scale to zero again. Add the sifted and whole-wheat flours. Using your hands and a bowl scraper, gently mix until all the flour is just a little wet (see Step 2 of the Master Formula, page 55). If the dough is shaggy and dry, add more water from your extra stash by dipping your hands in the water and continuing to mix until it is slightly sticky.

Cover with cheesecloth or a linen napkin and let rest for 40 minutes.

Continued . . .

Working in batches, sprinkle 5 g of the salt over the top of the dough (see Step 3 of the Master Formula, page 58). Moisten hands by dipping them in your reserve water stash and slowly massage the dough until the salt granules have dissolved into the mixture. Use a bowl scraper to fold the dough over and onto itself. Add 5 g more of the salt, mixing until dissolved. Add the remaining 4 g salt and mix until dissolved completely, dipping your hands in the water as needed.

Transfer the dough from the bowl to a shallow square plastic container, cover loosely with cheesecloth or a linen napkin, and let sit for 30 minutes in a warm place.

Use your hands to dig down and reach the bottom of the dough (see Step 4 of the Master Formula, page 59). Gently lift and pull (don't tear) the dough and fold it over itself. Work each side like this until the dough has been lifted and folded 4 times. Let sit, loosely covered, for 30 minutes. Repeat the process for a second turn, but add half of the Parmesan and garlic on top of the dough. Fold one side of the dough over the filling. Add the remaining Parmesan and garlic and fold the dough over again. Let sit, covered, for 30 minutes. Repeat the process for a third, fourth, and fifth turn and let sit, covered, for 30 minutes after each turn. Perform the sixth turn and let sit, covered, for 30 minutes.

Divide (or bake as Pan Bread, see page 79), shape, sleep, and bake the dough as instructed in Steps 5 through 8 of the Heritage Bread Master Formula (pages 61 through 65). See Step 9 for serving and storage (page 68).

NOTE

To roast the garlic, preheat the oven to 350°F [175°C]. Slice the top off of a bulb of garlic. Place the bulb on a piece of aluminum foil, drizzle with olive oil, wrap in the foil, and roast until soft and caramelized, about 25 minutes. Gently squeeze the soft cloves from the papery skins. Mince 10 g to use in the recipe.

PICHOLINE OLIVE

MAKES 2 LOAVES

135 g starter (page 47)

500 g water, plus 30 g as needed (76°F to 78°F [24.5°C to 25.5°C])

510 g sifted heritage flour (HRW/HRS), such as Glenn, Turkey Red, or Red Fife

200 g heritage whole-wheat flour (HRW/HRS), such as Glenn, Turkey Red, or Marquis

14 g fine sea salt

100 g pitted Picholine olives, halved

1 g chopped fresh thyme

1 g chopped fresh rosemary

1 g dried or chopped fresh oregano

5 g extra-virgin olive oil

Green olives have a firmer, denser texture than black olives because they're picked before ripening, which helps them stand up to the heat in bread baking. The Picholine olive is richer and more buttery than other types, but if you prefer another kind of green olive or even a black olive, you can use it instead. Just know that the olives might be softer once baked. I also prefer to use fresh herbs, but those are harder to source during our midwestern winters.

Feed and rest your starter (see Step 1 of the Master Formula, page 54).

Once the starter is ready, set a large bowl on the scale. Weigh out 500 g of water. Measure the 30 g reserve water and set aside.

Return the bowl of water to the scale and tare the scale to zero. Add the starter and, using your hand, dissolve it gently in the water.

Tare the scale to zero again. Add the sifted and whole-wheat flours. Using your hands and a bowl scraper, gently mix until all the flour is just a little wet (see Step 2 of the Master Formula, page 55). If the dough is shaggy and dry, add more water from your extra stash by dipping your hands in the water and continuing to mix until it is slightly sticky.

Cover with cheesecloth or a linen napkin and let rest for 40 minutes.

Continued . . .

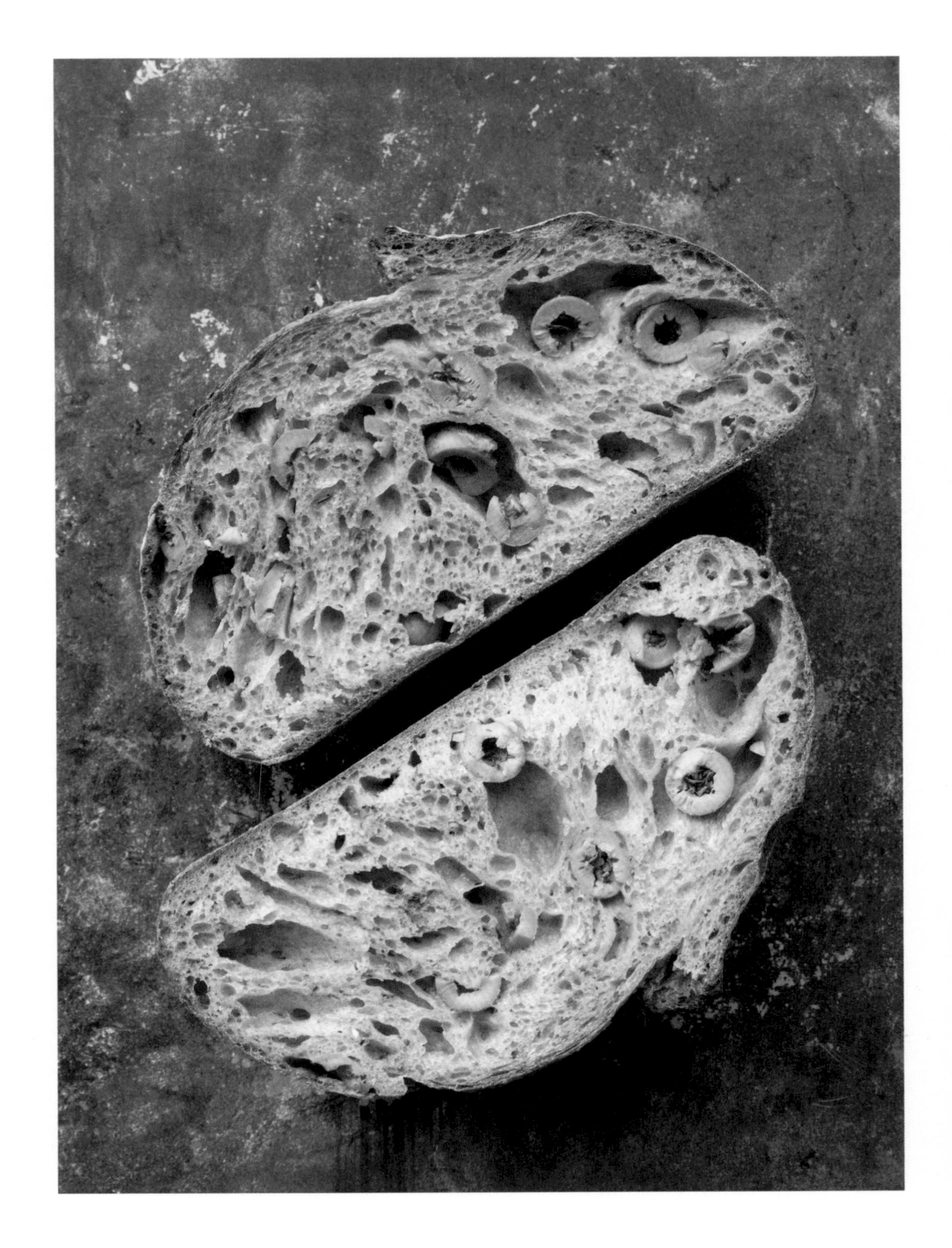

Working in batches, sprinkle 5 g of the salt over the top of the dough (see Step 3 of the Master Formula, page 58). Moisten hands by dipping them in your reserve water stash and slowly massage the dough until the salt granules have dissolved into the mixture. Use a bowl scraper to fold the dough over and onto itself. Add 5 g more of the salt, mixing until dissolved. Add the remaining 4 g salt and mix until dissolved completely, dipping your hands in the water as needed.

Transfer the dough from the bowl to a shallow square plastic container, cover loosely with cheesecloth or a linen napkin, and let sit for 30 minutes in a warm place.

While the dough rests, in a medium bowl, mix together the olives, thyme, rosemary, oregeno, and olive oil. Add the mixture to the top of dough after it has rested. Use your hands to dig down and reach the bottom of the dough (see Step 4 of the Master Formula, page 59). Gently lift and pull (don't tear) the dough and fold it over itself. Work each side like this until the dough has been lifted and folded 4 times. Let sit, loosely covered, for 30 minutes. Repeat the process for a second, third, fourth, and fifth turn and let sit, covered, for 30 minutes after each turn. Perform the sixth turn and let sit, covered, for 30 minutes.

Divide (or bake as Pan Bread, see page 79), shape, sleep, and bake the dough as instructed in Steps 5 through 8 of the Heritage Bread Master Formula (pages 61 through 65). See Step 9 for serving and storage (page 68).

CRANBERRY WALNUT

MAKES 2 LOAVES

135 g starter (page 47)

500 g water, plus 30 g as needed (76°F to 78°F [24.5°C to 25.5°C])

510 g sifted heritage flour, such as Red Fife or Marquis

200 g heritage whole-wheat flour (HRW/HRS), such as Turkey Red, Rouge de Bordeaux, or Glenn

14 g fine sea salt

75 g unsweetened dried cranberries

150 g walnuts, toasted and chopped

10 g walnut oil

I am normally not a fan of fruit breads, but customers always asked for them, so I knew we had to offer something. Ever since I studied in Maine, I've felt more of a kinship with the cranberry than the raisin. Cranberries are one of the three native fruits to North America (the others are blueberries and Concord grapes). In the nineteenth and early twentieth centuries, Maine was a large producer of cranberries. Today, Wisconsin is a leading producer of cranberries. Using walnut oil not only tenderizes the dough, but it also adds a highly addictive and earthy richness to the bread. You've been warned: eating a whole loaf by yourself is wonderfully possible.

Feed and rest your starter (see Step 1 of the Master Formula, page 54).

Once the starter is ready, set a large bowl on the scale. Weigh out 500 g of water. Measure the 30 g of reserve water and set aside.

Return the bowl of water to the scale and tare the scale to zero. Add the starter and, using your hand, dissolve it gently in the water.

Tare the scale to zero again. Add the sifted and whole-wheat flours. Using your hands and a bowl scraper, gently mix until all the flour is just a little wet (see Step 2 of the Master Formula, page 55). If the dough is shaggy and dry, add more water from your extra stash by dipping your hands in the water and continuing to mix until it is slightly sticky.

Cover with cheesecloth or a linen napkin and let rest for 40 minutes.

Continued . . .

Working in batches, sprinkle 5 g of the salt over the top of the dough (see Step 3 of the Master Formula, page 58). Moisten hands by dipping them in your reserve water stash and slowly massage the dough until the salt granules have dissolved into the mixture. Use a bowl scraper to fold the dough over and onto itself. Add 5 g more of the salt, mixing until dissolved. Add the remaining 4 g salt and mix until dissolved completely, dipping your hands in the water as needed.

Transfer the dough from the bowl to a shallow square plastic container, cover loosely with cheesecloth or a linen napkin, and let sit for 30 minutes in a warm place.

While the dough rests, in a medium bowl, mix together the cranberries, walnuts, and walnut oil. Add the mixture to the top of the dough after it has rested. Use your hands to dig down and reach the bottom of the dough (see Step 4 of the Master Formula, page 59). Gently lift and pull (don't tear) the dough and fold it over itself. Work each side like this until the dough has been lifted and folded 4 times. Let sit, loosely covered, for 30 minutes. Repeat the process for a second, third, fourth, and fifth turn and let sit, covered, for 30 minutes after each turn. Perform the sixth turn and let sit, covered, for 30 minutes.

Divide (or bake as Pan Bread, see page 79), shape, sleep, and bake the dough as instructed in Steps 5 through 8 of the Heritage Bread Master Formula (pages 61 through 65). See Step 9 for serving and storage (page 68).

POTATO ROSEMARY

MAKES 2 LOAVES

150 g heirloom potatoes (such as Kennebec, German Butterball, or Purple Viking), unpeeled and diced

5 g olive oil

5 g chopped fresh rosemary

3 g garlic powder (optional)

135 g starter (page 47)

500 g water, plus 30 g as needed (76°F to 78°F [24.5°C to 25.5°C])

510 g sifted heritage flour (HRW/HRS), such as Turkey Red

200 g heritage whole-wheat flour (HRW/HRS), such as Red Fife

14 g fine sea salt

The herbaceous smell of this bread will fill your whole house when it's baking. Start by picking an interesting heirloom variety of potato at the farmers' market. I've used Kennebec, German Butterball, and Purple Viking. Yukon gold works, too. Because I use skin-on diced potatoes, you will see little golden or purple cubes throughout the bread when you cut into the baked loaf. You don't have to roast the potatoes until they are completely tender because they will cook more as the bread bakes.

Preheat the oven to 350°F [180°C]. In a large bowl, toss the potatoes with the olive oil, rosemary, and garlic powder (if using). Spread into a single layer on a rimmed baking sheet. Bake for 15 minutes, or until the potatoes are just tender and beginning to brown. Remove from the oven and let cool.

Feed and rest your starter (see Step 1 of the Master Formula, page 54).

Once the starter is ready, set a large bowl on the scale. Weigh out 500 g of water. Measure the 30 g of reserve water and set aside.

Return the bowl of water to the scale and tare the scale to zero. Add the starter and, using your hand, dissolve it gently in the water.

Tare the scale to zero again. Add the sifted and whole-wheat flours. Using your hands and a bowl scraper, gently mix until all the flour is just a little wet (see Step 2 of the Master Formula, page 55). If the dough is shaggy and dry, add

Continued . . .

more water from your extra stash by dipping your hands in the water and continuing to mix until it is slightly sticky.

Cover with cheesecloth or a linen napkin and let rest for 40 minutes.

Working in batches, sprinkle 5 g of the salt over the top of the dough (see Step 3 of the Master Formula, page 58). Moisten hands by dipping them in your reserve water stash and slowly massage the dough until the salt granules have dissolved into the mixture. Use a bowl scraper to fold the dough over and onto itself. Add 5 g more of the salt, mixing until dissolved. Add the remaining 4 g salt and mix until dissolved completely, dipping your hands in the water as needed.

Transfer the dough from the bowl to a shallow square plastic container, cover loosely with cheesecloth or a linen napkin, and let sit for 30 minutes in a warm place.

Add the potato mixture to the top of the dough after it has rested. Use your hands to dig down and reach the bottom of the dough (see Step 4 of the Master Formula, page 59). Gently lift and pull (don't tear) the dough and fold it over itself. Work each side like this until the dough has been lifted and folded 4 times. Let sit, loosely covered, for 30 minutes. Repeat the process for a second, third, fourth, and fifth turn and let sit, covered, for 30 minutes after each turn. Perform the sixth turn and let sit, covered, for 30 minutes.

Divide (or bake as Pan Bread, see page 79), shape, sleep, and bake the dough as instructed in Steps 5 through 8 of the Heritage Bread Master Formula (pages 61 through 65). See Step 9 for serving and storage (page 68).

ANDY HAZZARD'S MARQUIS WHEAT

by Amelia Levin

ANDY HAZZARD'S AMBER-HUED dreadlocks shimmer in the sun, picking up the copper tips of the wheat stalks growing taller by the day.

"This is it," she says, pointing to the three 150-foot-long rows of her prized Marquis wheat. We grow quiet, enough to hear the "shh" sound as the wind blows over the tops of the shaggy green and golden carpet, creating gently rolling waves like Lake Michigan.

Ellen's eyes widen. She's downright giddy when she whips out her camera to snap some photos of Andy standing—almost blending into—the landscape of her wheat.

This really is their "baby." A very slow-growing baby at that.

Remnants of the burned-out tractor and barn from a devastating fire that took hold earlier that spring lie nearby, further proof that anything goes when you're growing wheat like in the olden days. Andy's family also sadly lost her mother's collection of photos and memorabilia in that fire, but the wheat and other crops were spared.

We're not at Andy's Hazzard Free Farm, in Pecatonica, Illinois, however; this is her father's fourth-generation conventional farm where Andy was able to borrow some space amid the cornfields to test out the Marquis wheat. If the Great Midwestern Bread Project flourishes, however, she'll create more space back on her farm.

The project all started with a sustainable food festival in Chicago. "Andy had a table of her purple barley, different colored heritage corn, and other beautiful grains, and I was instantly drawn there," Ellen says, recalling how they first met. "We started talking and hit it off right away. Andy had some ancient emmer grains, but I asked her if she would ever want to try growing heritage wheat varieties."

Turns out, Andy had already been considering that possibility given the then-recent activity on the West Coast, where scientists and farmers were researching and redeveloping varieties growing in the United States more than 100 years ago. She just needed a committed buyer.

Together the pair scoured farm journals and bulletins archived by the University of Wisconsin that detailed different types of heritage wheat grown throughout the Midwest and specifically in Andy's region of Illinois, which is halfway between the east and west state lines.

They settled on the Marquis, a natural hybrid historically grown in this region, but which fell out of favor during the Green Revolution, when large mills preferred higher-yield crops.

Based on the characteristics of the wheat and Andy's immediate climate, they knew there was a chance the seeds could survive, especially because these were hard spring wheat seeds, meaning they would be planted after the harsh winter in March or April and harvested later in the summer.

Andy reached out to a handful of farmers and seed savers in her network, looking for the seeds, eventually getting her hands on 2.2 pounds, or 1 kilo, of wheat from a college professor.

After the first season, Andy was able to save 30 pounds of the crop for seed. All of it went back into the field, so Ellen would have to wait another year—possibly two—before she could use any for flour. Even three years into the Great Midwestern Bread Project (at press time), Andy had been able to harvest only enough wheat for just 10 pounds of flour, harvested in the hot summer sun with scissors because the huge combine would destroy the smaller crop and even Andy's family's farm tools like her scythe weren't available, having been destroyed in that fire. This harvest amounted to just five test loaves. "The Marquis loaves, in my opinion, taste like a strong whole wheat, but with a very nutty flavor that takes on the sourdough starter really well," Ellen says.

Next year, they hope to harvest more wheat berries that Andy will "clean" using her gravity table to screen out impurities, and then process into flour using her small stone mill. If her harvest continues to expand, they'll need to partner with a larger artisan miller in the region.

Clearly, growing heritage wheat is a time-tested and risky feat; if growing commodity wheat is a marathon, growing heritage wheat is the ultramarathon, she says. But the reward is worth the enduring effort; Andy and Ellen are sowing, growing, and baking for the future.

"I didn't want to grow conventional corn that was just going to go to animal feed; I wanted to grow something healthy and nutritious that people can actually eat."

Back at Andy's circa-1847 farm, we help her pick raspberries off the overflowing bush in the front yard. Ellen is saving some to bake into her berry muffins back at Hewn, but not before we each eat about a pound's worth of the sweet and tart, low-hanging fruit staining our lips. It's moments like these that remind Andy why she grows what she does.

"I didn't want to grow conventional corn that was just going to go to animal feed; I wanted to grow something healthy and nutritious that people can actually eat," she says in between bites of the raspberries.

A degree holder in agricultural science, urban forestry, and native restoration from Western Illinois University, Andy started off with her own greenhouse and high-end landscaping business focused on native restoration. But the use of chemicals bothered her, and she just got burned out. She switched to growing heirloom vegetables using organic practices and has since moved into corn and grains. "I wanted to bring my spiritual, philosophical, and ecological views all together, and farming just does that for me," she says.

"Yes, but you are the one in your family farming and doing it in the hardest possible way," Ellen reminds her.

Later we say hi to the goats, chickens, cats, and dogs milling about the grounds, where she hosts regular farm dinners with Ellen and chefs every year. In just a couple of weeks, she would host her first grain summit, bringing in millers and farmers from the area to discuss the forward movement of heritage grain growing in this country.

Andy's farm looks how farms did back in the 1800s, set along a creek lined with trees and natural greenery and small plots of land where different types of vegetables, grains, and crops are rotated around to keep the soil healthy and nitrogen-rich. The animals and bugs and dirt and plants all have their place, their job in keeping everything working together in sync and in the circle of life. It's not an easy way to farm or make a living, Andy admits, but it's the real way. There are no chemicals here.

On our way out, Ellen picks up a bag of Andy's stone-rolled oats she milled just the day before. Ellen will use those for her Morning Glory Muffins (page 164) at the bakery. The bag of rusty red–colored Bloody Butcher polenta and finely ground Floriani Flint cornmeal will go to cornbread (page 153) and other uses.

The more Ellen buys, the more Andy can plant and get closer to her goal of "healing the land," as she puts it. And as that land continues to heal, the more that Marquis wheat will grow, and the more great bread we'll have to eat. That's the heritage way.

SPENT GRAIN BREAD

MAKES 2 LOAVES

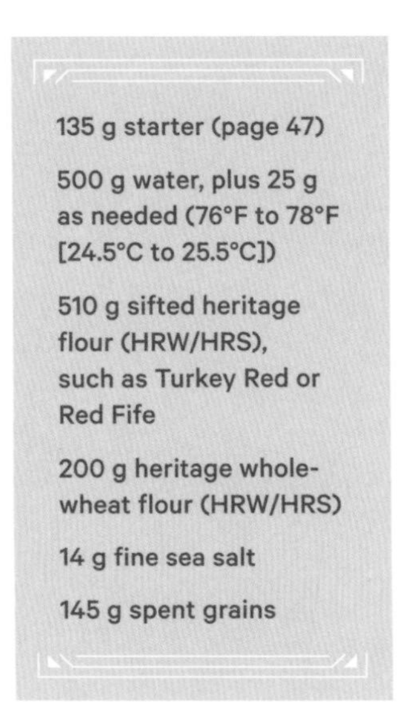

135 g starter (page 47)

500 g water, plus 25 g as needed (76°F to 78°F [24.5°C to 25.5°C])

510 g sifted heritage flour (HRW/HRS), such as Turkey Red or Red Fife

200 g heritage whole-wheat flour (HRW/HRS)

14 g fine sea salt

145 g spent grains

There are several local breweries in Evanston that started brewing beer around the same time we started baking bread. One day, a local brewer asked if we could find a way to use their spent grain, which is the leftover grain berries after the sugars and protein have been used up in the brewing process. If you want to try this bread out, we suggest you make friends with a local brewery and ask for a bag of about 300 g worth of their spent grain. Most breweries either compost or discard the spent grains, so they should be happy to give you some!

Once you acquire the grains, use your hands to squeeze out as much liquid as you can over a bowl, then let the grains drain in a colander for 30 minutes. The spent grains give the bread a very soft crumb and there's a slight chewiness every now and then when you hit a berry. It does not taste like beer, but you get some added fiber from the spent grain. Note that we have reduced the reserve water needed for this recipe to account for the extra moisture in the spent grain.

Feed and rest your starter (see Step 1 of the Master Formula, page 54).

Once the starter is ready, set a large bowl on the scale. Weigh out 500 g of water. Measure the 25 g of reserve water and set aside.

Return the bowl of water to the scale and tare the scale to zero. Add the starter and, using your hand, dissolve it gently in the water.

Continued . . .

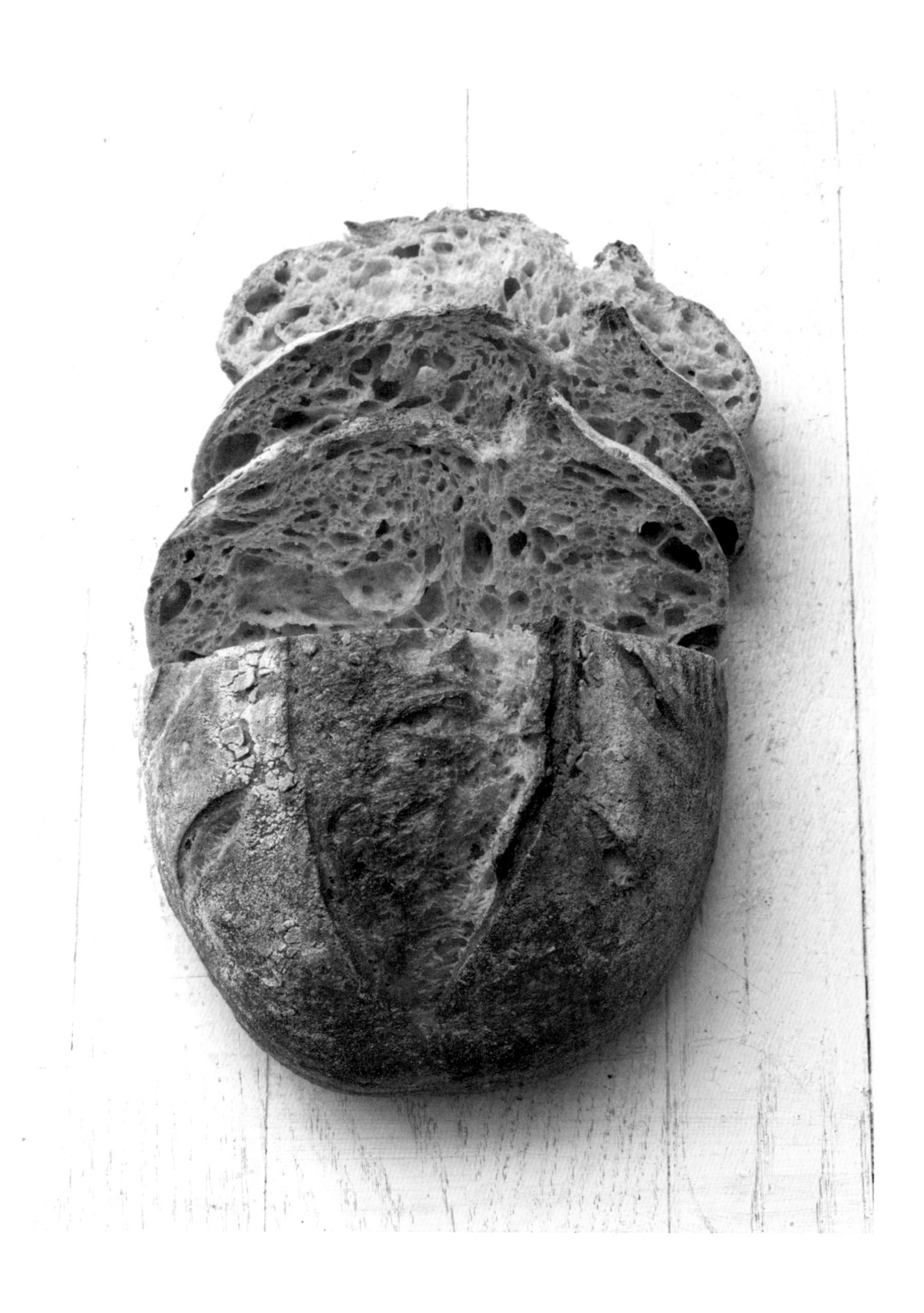

Tare the scale to zero again. Add the sifted and whole-wheat flours. Using your hands and a bowl scraper, gently mix until all the flour is just a little wet (see Step 2 of the Master Formula, page 55). If the dough is shaggy and dry, add more water from your extra stash by dipping your hands in the water and continuing to mix until it is slightly sticky.

Cover with cheesecloth or a linen napkin and let rest for 40 minutes.

Working in batches, sprinkle 5 g of the salt over the top of the dough (see Step 3 of the Master Formula, page 58). Moisten hands by dipping them in your reserve water stash and slowly massage the dough until the salt granules have dissolved into the mixture. Use a bowl scraper to fold the dough over and onto itself. Add 5 g more of the salt, mixing until dissolved. Add the remaining 4 g salt and mix until dissolved completely, dipping your hands in the water as needed.

Transfer the dough from the bowl to a shallow square plastic container, cover loosely with cheesecloth or a linen napkin, and let sit for 30 minutes in a warm place.

Add the spent grains to the top of the dough after it has rested. Use your hands to dig down and reach the bottom of the dough (see Step 4 of the Master Formula, page 59). Gently lift and pull (don't tear) the dough and fold it over itself. Work each side like this until the dough has been lifted and folded 4 times. Let sit, loosely covered, for 30 minutes. Repeat the process for a second, third, fourth, and fifth turn and let sit, covered, for 30 minutes after each turn. Perform the sixth turn and let sit, covered, for 30 minutes.

Divide (or bake as Pan Bread, see page 79), shape, sleep, and bake the dough as instructed in Steps 5 through 8 of the Heritage Bread Master Formula (pages 61 through 65). See Step 9 for serving and storage (page 68).

HERITAGE FLATBREAD

MAKES 2 FLATBREADS

DOUGH (IF NOT USING LEFTOVER HERITAGE COUNTRY BREAD DOUGH

135 g starter (page 47)

500 g water (76°F to 78°F [24.5°C to 25.5°C]), plus 30 g as needed

510 g sifted heritage flour (HRW/HRS), such as Glenn

200 g heritage whole-wheat flour (HRW/HRS), such as Rouge de Bordeaux or Turkey Red

14 g fine sea salt

FLATBREAD

75 g (¼ cup) coarse-milled heritage cornmeal (polenta)

50 g (¼ cup) olive oil

1 g (¼ tsp) fine sea salt

1 g (¼ tsp) freshly ground black pepper

2 heirloom tomatoes, thinly sliced (optional)

120 g (1 cup) shredded fresh mozzarella (optional)

Sliced fresh basil, for garnish (optional)

Every Friday, we make flatbread at the bakery. It is fun to use our country bread dough in a different way, and it allows us to be more creative with savory ingredients. Depending on the season, we rotate our flatbreads each week to match the vegetables that are available. In the summer, for example, when tomatoes are in season, we always make a Margherita-style flatbread. But you can add any toppings you want, such as chopped peppers, roasted garlic, and goat cheese, or cooked beets with Parmesan and blue cheese or pesto—just cook until the toppings are bubbly. Our flatbread dough holds up really well in the oven, but make sure to brush it with olive oil before adding any topping to protect it from burning. A little oil also helps crisp up the crust. You will need a pizza peel and pizza stone.

Use 1 recipe leftover Heritage Country bread dough (page 70), or start the process to make that dough, detailed below.

To make the dough, feed and rest your starter (see Step 1 of the Master Formula, page 54).

Once the starter is ready, set a large bowl on the scale. Weigh out 500 g of water. Measure the 30 g of reserve water and set aside.

Return the bowl of water to the scale and tare the scale to zero. Add the starter and, using your hand, dissolve it gently in the water.

Tare the scale to zero again. Add the sifted and whole-wheat flours. Using your hands and a bowl scraper, gently mix until

Continued . . .

all the flour is just a little wet (see Step 2 of the Master Formula, page 55). If the dough is shaggy and dry, add more water from your extra stash by dipping your hands in the water and continuing to mix until it is slightly sticky.

Cover with cheesecloth or a linen napkin and let rest for 40 minutes.

Working in batches, sprinkle 6 g of the salt over the top of the dough (see Step 3 of the Master Formula, page 58). Moisten hands by dipping them in your reserve water stash and slowly massage the dough until the salt granules have dissolved into the mixture. Use a bowl scraper to fold the dough over and onto itself. Add 6 g more of the salt, mixing until dissolved. Add the remaining 2 g salt and mix until dissolved completely, dipping your hands in the water as needed.

Transfer the dough from the bowl to a shallow plastic container, cover loosely with cheesecloth or a linen napkin, and let sit for 30 minutes in a warm place.

Use your hands to dig down and reach the bottom of the dough (see Step 4 of the Master Formula, page 59). Gently lift and pull (don't tear) the dough and fold it over itself. Work each side like this until the dough has been lifted and folded 4 times. Let sit, loosely covered, for 30 minutes. Repeat the process for a second, third, fourth, and fifth turn and let sit, covered, for 30 minutes after each turn. Perform the sixth turn and let sit, covered, for 30 minutes.

Place a pizza stone in the oven and preheat the oven to 475°F [240°C].

Meanwhile, to make the flatbread, divide the dough into two balls. Take one of the dough balls and use a rolling pin to roll into an oval that's ½ in [12 mm] thick. Refrigerate or freeze the remaining dough ball for future use, or shape and bake it after baking the first flatbread.

Continue to roll out the dough until the oval is about 14 by 10 in [35.5 by 25 cm]. Sprinkle a wooden or steel pizza peel or the bottom of a rimmed baking sheet with coarse cornmeal; this will help the dough slide onto a pizza stone. Place the rolled-out dough on the pizza peel or the bottom of a baking sheet.

Brush the dough with olive oil and sprinkle with the salt and pepper. Lay the tomatoes over the dough and sprinkle with the mozzarella (if using). Carefully slide the dough onto the pizza stone.

Bake for 10 minutes, or until the bottom is just set. Rotate and bake 5 minutes more, or until the crust is golden and the cheese is bubbly. Sprinkle with basil (if using). Cut into wedges (or other slices) and serve immediately.

BLOODY BUTCHER POLENTA BREAD

MAKES 2 LOAVES

PORRIDGE

75 g (½ cup) boiling water

130 g coarse-milled heritage cornmeal (polenta), such as Bloody Butcher or another dent variety

10 g chopped fresh thyme

50 g pumpkin seeds, lightly toasted

DOUGH

135 g starter (page 47)

475 g water, plus 25 g as needed (76°F to 78°F [24.5°C to 25.5°C])

510 g sifted heritage flour (HRW/HRS), such as Red Fife or Glenn

200 g heritage whole-wheat flour (HRW/HRS), such as Rouge de Bordeaux or Turkey Red

14 g fine sea salt

Living in the Midwest, it is a given that we have access to a lot of corn. Sadly, most of the corn grown here is used for animal feed or other uses that make them unsuitable for human consumption. I was first introduced to heirloom varieties of corn by Andy Hazzard of Hazzard Free Farm (see page 106). She grows Bloody Butcher corn along with a handful of other heritage corn varieties that look and taste great. This corn is a dent variety that has deep red kernels and flakes of yellow when milled into a coarse cornmeal. Andy discovered records showing that Bloody Butcher has been grown since the early 1840s. If you can't find Bloody Butcher, look for other heritage corn varieties in your region.

To make the porridge, bring the water to a boil in a small saucepan or kettle. Meanwhile, in a bowl, stir together the cornmeal and thyme. Pour the boiling water over the mixture, cover with aluminum foil, and let sit for 30 minutes.

Add the pumpkin seeds to the cornmeal mixture and stir until just combined. Set aside.

To make the dough, feed and rest your starter (see Step 1 of the Master Formula, page 54).

Once the starter is ready, set a large bowl on the scale. Weigh out 475 g of water. Measure the 25 g of reserve water and set aside.

Return the bowl of water to the scale and tare the scale to zero. Add the starter and, using your hand, dissolve it gently in the water.

Continued . . .

Tare the scale to zero again. Add the sifted and whole-wheat flours. Using your hands and a bowl scraper, gently mix until all the flour is just a little wet (see Step 2 of the Master Formula, page 55). If the dough is shaggy and dry, add more water from your extra stash by dipping your hands in the water and continuing to mix until it is slightly sticky.

Cover with cheesecloth or a linen napkin and let rest for 40 minutes.

Working in batches, sprinkle 6 g of the salt over the top of the dough (see Step 3 of the Master Formula, page 58). Moisten hands by dipping them in your reserve water stash and slowly massage the dough until the salt granules have dissolved into the mixture. Use a bowl scraper to fold the dough over and onto itself. Add 5 g more of the salt, mixing until dissolved. Add the remaining 3 g salt and mix until dissolved completely, dipping your hands in the water as needed.

Transfer the dough from the bowl to a shallow square plastic container, cover loosely with cheesecloth or a linen napkin, and let sit for 30 minutes in a warm place.

Add the cornmeal mixture to the top of the dough after it has rested. Use your hands to dig down and reach the bottom of the dough (see Step 4 of the Master Formula, page 59). Gently lift and pull (don't tear) the dough and fold it over itself. Work each side like this until the dough has been lifted and folded 4 times. Let sit, loosely covered, for 30 minutes. Repeat the process for a second, third, fourth, and fifth turn and let sit, covered, for 30 minutes after each turn. Perform the sixth turn and let sit, covered, for 30 minutes.

Divide (or bake as Pan Bread, see page 79), shape, sleep, and bake the dough as instructed in Steps 5 through 8 of the Heritage Bread Master Formula (pages 61 through 65). See Step 9 for serving and storage (page 68).

HERITAGE RYE

MAKES 2 LOAVES

CARAMELIZED ONION

10 g olive oil

1 yellow onion, diced

3 g anise seeds (optional)

DOUGH

125 g starter (page 47)

500 g water, plus 30 g as needed (88°F to 90°F [31°C to 32°C])

425 g heritage rye flour, such as Abruzzi, Danko, or Driftless rye

285 g sifted heritage flour (HRW/HRS), such as Turkey Red

14 g fine sea salt

While you're mixing the rye bread with your hands, you'll probably wonder why I've included this recipe. It becomes a heavy dough that coats your skin like concrete. But once baked, there is nothing better than a fresh loaf of rye. If you have extra time, adding caramelized onion rounds out the rye's floral, sharp flavor with some buttery notes. If you're not a huge fan of licorice, skip the anise seeds. We decided to add them to our rye bread when a European airline commissioned us to make bread for their flights from Chicago to Europe, and we loved the more complex taste. Rye grows really well in the cold Midwest, though it is considered a weed in some states. Oddly enough, rye works well with warmer water and a warmer room to bulk ferment in (85°F [29.5°C]). I love eating a hearty, earthy loaf of rye on a cold winter day. But it does take some fortitude to mix and shape this loaf, so do it on a day you're feeling mentally and physically strong.

—◆—

To make the caramelized onion, heat the olive oil in a large sauté pan over medium heat. Add the onion and cook for 15 minutes, or until tender and caramelized, stirring occasionally and lowering the heat as necessary to ensure the onions don't burn. Remove the pan from the heat. Let the onion cool completely.

Meanwhile, put the anise seeds (if using) in a small bowl. Add just enough boiling water to submerge the seeds. Set aside for 30 minutes and let cool completely. Drain the seeds before adding them to the caramelized onion.

To make the dough, feed and rest your starter (see Step 1 of the Master Formula, page 54).

Continued . . .

Once the starter is ready, set a large bowl on the scale. Weigh out 500 g of water. Measure the 30 g of reserve water and set aside.

Return the bowl of water to the scale and tare the scale to zero. Add the starter and, using your hand, dissolve it gently in the water.

Tare the scale to zero again. Add the rye and sifted flours. Using your hands and a bowl scraper, gently mix until all the flour is just a little wet (see Step 2 of the Master Formula, page 55). If the dough is shaggy and dry, add more water from your extra stash by dipping your hands in the water and continuing to mix until it is slightly sticky.

Cover with cheesecloth or a linen napkin and let rest for 40 minutes.

Working in batches, sprinkle 5 g of the salt over the top of the dough (see Step 3 of the Master Formula, page 58). Moisten hands by dipping them in your reserve water stash and slowly massage the dough until the salt granules have dissolved into the mixture. Use a bowl scraper to fold the dough over and onto itself. Add 5 g more of the salt, mixing until dissolved. Add the remaining 4 g salt and mix until dissolved completely, dipping your hands in the water as needed.

Transfer the dough from the bowl to a 2-in [5-cm] square plastic container, cover loosely with cheesecloth or a linen napkin, and let sit for 30 minutes in a warm place.

Add the caramelized onion mixture to the top of the dough after it has rested. Use your hands to dig down and reach the bottom of the dough (see Step 4 of the Master Formula, page 59). Gently lift and pull (don't tear) the dough and fold it over itself. Work each side like this until the dough has been lifted and folded 4 times. Let sit, loosely covered, for 30 minutes. Repeat the process for a second, third, fourth, and fifth turn and let sit, covered, for 30 minutes after each turn. Perform the sixth turn and let sit, covered, for 30 minutes.

Divide (or bake as Pan Bread, see page 79), shape, sleep, and bake the dough as instructed in Steps 5 through 8 of the Heritage Bread Master Formula (pages 61 through 65). See Step 9 for serving and storage (page 68).

CHAPTER THREE

ENRICHED HERITAGE BREADS

BASIC BRIOCHE DOUGH

**MAKES ENOUGH FOR 2 LOAVES
OR ABOUT 15 FLAVORED ROLLS**

100 g (½ cup) whole milk

200 g (4 large) eggs

430 g (3 cups) sifted heritage flour (HRS/HRW), such as Rouge de Bordeaux or Glenn

70 g (⅓ cup) sugar

16 g (1½ tsp) fine sea salt

5 g (1 tsp) instant yeast

227 g (1 cup) cold unsalted high-fat butter (such as Plugra), cut into small cubes

Brioche is one of the most versatile doughs. At Hewn, we use brioche dough to make sweet or savory pastries as well as traditional loaves that can be sliced for French toast or a decadent grilled cheese. It's also delicious when served warm and slathered with a really good jam. I think of this recipe as a sensible midwestern brioche because I use locally grown wheat, even though historically, brioche was enjoyed by kings and queens in France. We use a heritage hard red winter or spring wheat, such as Rouge de Bordeaux or Glenn, which both have a very delicate wheat flavor and silky texture.

Some brioche recipes call for up to 90 percent butter. But since we are a little more modest in the Midwest (and because I prefer a lighter bread), we stick with 50 percent butter at the bakery, although the European-style butter we use has a higher butterfat percentage. Note that this recipe requires the dough to be chilled for about an hour before shaping. I also highly recommend using a stand mixer instead of your hands because the dough gets really thick and hard to handle. In fact, don't be surprised how long it might take to mix completely. Also, although I'm a huge proponent of natural starters, we use a little instant yeast in the brioche. The instant yeast works better with the brioche, especially with the recipes that have added sugar. It allows a quicker, more consistent proof and bake.

In the stand mixer bowl set over a scale, pour in the milk until the scale reads 100 g. Crack the eggs and add to the same bowl. Set the bowl on the stand mixer with the dough hook attachment.

Continued . . .

Add the flour to the stand mixer mixture. Mix on medium speed until the dough is smooth and comes together, about 3 minutes, scraping down the bowl after the first minute of mixing.

Let the dough rest in the bowl for 20 minutes to help relax the gluten.

Add the sugar, salt, and yeast and mix on low speed for 3 minutes more, scraping the dough off the hook after the first minute.

Add half of the butter and continue to mix on low speed until the butter cubes are no longer visible and are completely incorporated into the dough. Add the remaining butter and mix until incorporated.

Once all the butter is added, mix the dough on medium speed until it makes a slapping sound and the dough comes away from the bowl, about 16 minutes. Resist the temptation to increase the speed. You will start hearing a distinct slapping sound when the dough is almost ready.

Coat a medium bowl with cooking spray and transfer the dough to the bowl to rest. Cover with plastic wrap and let stand at room temperature for 1 hour.

Punch down the dough to help redistribute the yeast. Cover the bowl with plastic wrap. Refrigerate for at least 2 hours or overnight.

After the dough has rested and chilled, choose any of the following recipes (pages 128 to 147) for shaping instructions, flavor additions, and baking time.

BRIOCHE LOAVES

MAKES 2 LOAVES

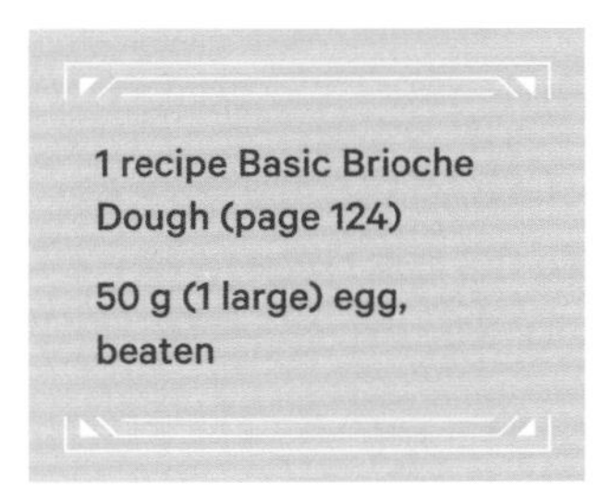
1 recipe Basic Brioche Dough (page 124)

50 g (1 large) egg, beaten

Coat a 9-by-4½-in [23-by-11-cm] loaf pan with cooking spray or butter. Divide the brioche dough in half, so you have two 600-g pieces. (Wrap and store the remaining dough in the refrigerator and use within the following 24 hours. If freezing, add 3 minutes to the final bake time. Save the extra baked brioche loaf for Bostock [page 131], if desired.)

Roll the brioche dough into an 8-by-4-in [20-by-10-cm] rectangle. Don't worry about making it exact. Roll the dough into a cylinder the length of the loaf pan. Gently roll the dough on a lightly floured wood surface in a football-like shape to create a tight skin on the top.

Use a bench scraper to lift the dough from the table and place the dough, seam-side down, into the loaf pan. The top should have a clean, tight surface.

Let proof, covered with plastic wrap, in a warm room for 2 to 2½ hours (if the air temperature is closer to 80°F [26.5°C]), or up to 3 hours in a cooler environment. When fully proofed, the center of the dough will rise to within ½ in [12 mm] of the top of the pan.

Preheat the oven to 375°F [190°C].

Brush the beaten egg over the top of the brioche and bake for 15 minutes. Rotate the pan, lower the temperature to 325°F [160°C], and continue to bake for 40 to 45 minutes, or until a thermometer inserted into the center reads 200°F [95°C].

Remove from the oven and run a knife along the edges of the pan. Carefully tip the loaf out of the pan immediately onto a wire rack to cool for 30 minutes before slicing to prevent sticking.

Cover the brioche in plastic wrap and it will keep for 2 days on the counter. Or chop up unused brioche and let dry out for 1 day, then chop with a food processor to use as bread crumbs.

BOSTOCK

MAKES 8 SLICES

1 Brioche Loaf (page 128)

FRANGIPANE

200 g (2 cups) toasted sliced almonds

100 g (½ cup) sugar

6 g (1 tsp) fine sea salt

226 g (1 cup) unsalted butter, cubed, at room temperature

100 g (2 large) eggs

20 g (2 Tbsp) bourbon

VANILLA SYRUP

200 g (1 cup) sugar

200 g (scant 2 cups) hot water

20 g (1 Tbsp) pure vanilla paste or extract

TOPPING

125 g (1 cup) sliced stone fruit or fresh berries

90 g (scant 1 cup) raw sliced almonds

Forget making French toast for your family; make bostock instead. Bostock is a French way of using day-old brioche and turning it into something fruity, nutty, and delicious. A customer of ours gave us a baking magazine from Australia and it had pictures of bostock. In thinking of how to put our spin on the recipe, we were inspired by seasonal fruit, like peaches and berries. Soaked in a vanilla bean syrup and topped with frangipane, bostock actually works best with an older, stale loaf of brioche—it's a great way to make sure your prized enriched bread doesn't go to waste.

Cut the brioche loaf into 8 slices.

To make the frangipane, put the almonds in a food processor and pulse until coarsely chopped. With the processor running, add the sugar and salt and process until just combined.

Add the butter in 3 additions and process until the butter is combined after each addition. Once all the butter is added, process until the mixture is light and fluffy. Add the eggs and process to combine. Drizzle in the bourbon and pulse 2 or 3 times until fully mixed. Refrigerate for at least 4 hours or overnight.

Preheat the oven to 350°F [175°C].

To make the vanilla syrup, stir together the sugar, water, and vanilla in a pie plate. Dip each bread slice into the syrup, soaking no longer than 10 seconds on each side to prevent the bread from getting too soggy.

Continued . . .

Place a wire rack over a rimmed baking sheet and arrange the brioche slices in a single layer. Top each slice with 55 g [¼ cup] of the frangipane, spreading it as if you were making a peanut butter sandwich. Top with 3 or 4 pieces of fruit or a small handful of berries and sprinkle with the raw almonds.

Bake for 25 to 30 minutes, or until the frangipane is golden and the fruit is cooked through. Let cool for 5 minutes and serve warm. These don't hold well for the next day, so plan to serve and eat within 4 hours of baking.

FETA-DILL BRIOCHE ROLLS

MAKES 15 ROLLS

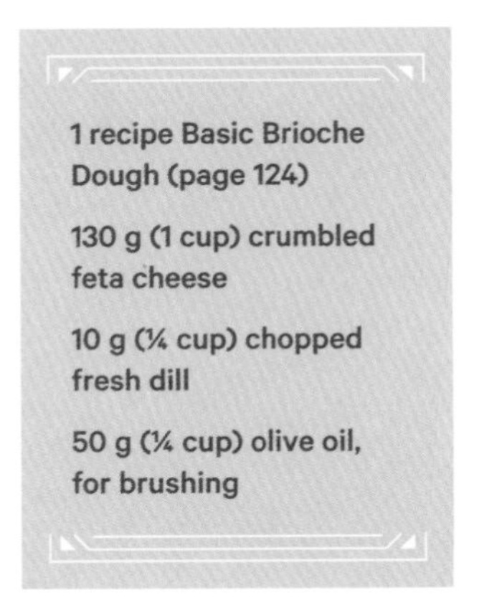

Our head baker, Justin, lived in Turkey for a few years and fell in love with Turkish baked goods. When he returned to the States, he started making these rolls, trying to re-create a favorite pastry he had there.

Divide the dough into fifteen 70-g pieces and shape into loose balls. Place the balls on a parchment paper–lined or oiled baking sheet, spacing them 2 to 3 in [5 to 7.5 cm] apart. Using the palm of your hand, flatten into ½-in- [12-mm-] thick discs.

Cover the dough pieces loosely with a large sheet of plastic wrap and let sit at room temperature for 1 hour to proof. The dough will rise by about ½ in [12 mm].

Preheat the oven to 350°F [175°C].

Combine the feta and dill in a small bowl. Using your two middle fingers, make a small indentation in each disc. Scoop 10 g (1 Tbsp) of the feta-dill mixture into each indentation.

Brush the tops and sides of the rolls with the olive oil. Bake for 10 minutes. Carefully rotate the baking sheet and bake for 5 to 7 minutes more, or until the edges are a deep golden brown.

Let cool for 5 minutes and serve warm. These don't taste as good the next day, so I recommend freezing the leftovers and warming in the oven at 325°F [160°C] for 5 minutes.

POTATO-ROSEMARY-GRUYÈRE BRIOCHE ROLLS

MAKES 15 ROLLS

300 g (2 or 3) small heirloom potatoes (such as Kennebec, German Butterball, or Yukon gold), unpeeled and diced

25 g (2 Tbsp) olive oil

4 g (1 tsp) chopped fresh rosemary

3 g (1 tsp) garlic powder

Pinch of fine sea salt

Pinch of freshly ground black pepper

1 recipe Basic Brioche Dough (page 124)

45 g (½ cup) shredded Gruyère cheese

We love finding interesting potatoes at the market and adding them to our brioche. This is a great savory pastry that works for breakfast or lunch.

Preheat the oven to 350°F [175°C]. Oil a baking sheet or line with parchment paper.

In a large bowl, toss the potatoes with the olive oil, rosemary, garlic powder, salt, and pepper. Spread into a single layer on the prepared baking sheet. Bake for 10 minutes, or until the potatoes are just tender and beginning to brown. Remove from the oven and let cool.

Divide the dough into fifteen 70-g pieces and shape into loose balls. Place the balls on the baking sheet, spacing them 2 to 3 in [5 to 7.5 cm] apart. Using the palm of your hand, flatten into ½-in- [12-mm-] thick discs.

Cover the dough pieces loosely with a large sheet of plastic wrap and let sit at room temperature for 1 hour to proof. The dough will almost double in size.

Preheat the oven again to 350°F [175°C]. Using two middle fingers, make a small indentation in each disc. Scoop about 20 g (2 Tbsp) of the potato mixture into each indentation and sprinkle with 3 g (1 tsp) of the cheese.

Bake the rolls for 10 minutes. Carefully rotate the baking sheet and bake for 5 to 7 minutes more, or until golden brown.

Let cool for 5 minutes and serve warm. These don't taste as good the next day, so I recommend freezing the leftovers and warming in the oven at 325°F [160°C] for 5 minutes.

SEASONAL BERRY BRIOCHE ROLLS

MAKES 15 ROLLS

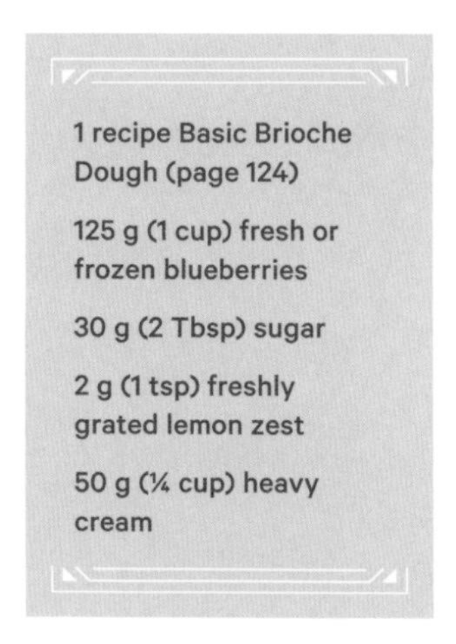

1 recipe Basic Brioche Dough (page 124)

125 g (1 cup) fresh or frozen blueberries

30 g (2 Tbsp) sugar

2 g (1 tsp) freshly grated lemon zest

50 g (¼ cup) heavy cream

Brioche and fruit—what could be more perfect? We try to find as many ways as possible to incorporate seasonal fruit into our recipes, especially as the weather warms up after a long and cold midwestern winter. Pick your favorite fruit and chop them into bite-size pieces for this recipe. We have found that blueberries, strawberries, and raspberries work the best.

Oil a baking sheet or line with parchment paper.

Divide the dough into fifteen 70-g pieces and shape into loose balls. Place the balls on the baking sheet, spacing them 2 to 3 in [5 to 7.5 cm] apart.

Using the palm of your hand, flatten into ½-in [12-mm-] thick saucers.

Cover the dough pieces loosely with a large sheet of plastic wrap and let sit at room temperature for 1 hour to proof. The dough will rise by about ½ in [12 mm].

Preheat the oven to 350°F [175°C].

Combine the blueberries, sugar, and lemon zest in a medium bowl. Using your two middle fingers, make a small indentation in each saucer. Scoop 10 g (1 Tbsp) of the berry mixture into each indentation and drizzle with 5 g (1 tsp) of the cream.

Bake for 15 minutes. If using frozen fruit, bake for 2 minutes more. Carefully rotate the baking sheet and bake for 10 minutes more, or until golden brown.

Let cool for 5 minutes and serve warm. These don't taste as good the next day, so I recommend freezing leftovers and warming in the oven at 325°F [160°C] for 5 minutes.

HOUSE JAM BRIOCHE ROLLS

MAKES 15 ROLLS

1 recipe Basic Brioche Dough (page 124)

160 g (½ cup) your favorite homemade or store-bought jam

50 g (1 large) egg, beaten

50 g (¼ cup) turbinado sugar

We love making jam at Hewn. Spencer, our head pastry chef, has a tradition of playing "Pump Up the Jam," and we all sing and dance while helping make the jam, which can take some time. We reward ourselves at the end of the long jam-making process with these delicious treats, which are a great way to enjoy the extra jam before canning or freezing.

Butter or oil 15 fluted brioche tins or standard muffin cups.

Divide the dough into fifteen 70-g pieces and shape into loose balls. Let rest on the counter for 5 to 10 minutes.

Using the palm of your hand, flatten into ¼-in- [6-mm-] thick saucers. Scoop 10 g (1 tsp) of the jam in the middle of each saucer. Fold the dough over the jam like a taco and seal the edges. Roll into a ball so the jam is nestled securely in the middle. Try not to roll so tightly that the jam breaks through the top.

Place the rolls seam-side down in the brioche tins or muffin cups. Cover loosely with plastic wrap and let sit at room temperature for 1 hour to proof. The dough will rise by about ½ inch [12 mm].

Preheat the oven to 350°F [175°C].

Brush the tops of the rolls with the beaten egg and sprinkle evenly with the sugar. Bake for 15 minutes. Rotate the pans and bake for 10 minutes more, or until golden brown.

Let cool for 5 minutes and serve warm. These don't taste as good the next day, so I recommend freezing the leftovers and warming in the oven at 325°F [160°C] for 5 minutes.

CINNAMON ROLL BRIOCHE

MAKES 15 ROLLS

1 recipe Basic Brioche Dough (page 124)

113 g (½ cup) unsalted butter, at room temperature

100 g (½ cup) lightly packed light brown sugar

1 g (¼ tsp) fine sea salt

9 g (1 heaping Tbsp) ground Ceylon cinnamon

6 g (1 Tbsp) freshly grated orange zest

100 g (2 large) eggs, beaten

10 g (1 heaping Tbsp) sifted heritage flour (SWS), such as Richland or White Sonora

25 g (2 Tbsp) turbinado sugar (optional)

ICING (OPTIONAL)

70 g (½ cup) confectioners' sugar

14 g (1 Tbsp) whole milk

I have had more cinnamon rolls in my day than I care to admit, but this one takes the cake, no pun intended. I like to use Ceylon cinnamon because it has a more delicate and sweeter, less bitter or acidic taste. Additionally, it is lower in coumarin, which in higher doses can actually be toxic and act as a blood thinner.

Roll the brioche dough into a 10-by-6-in [25-by-15-cm] rectangle on a lightly floured cutting board or counter. Chill briefly in the refrigerator while preparing the rest of the ingredients.

In a large bowl, whisk together the butter, brown sugar, salt, cinnamon, orange zest, 1 of the eggs, and flour until creamy.

Using a rolling pin, roll the dough into a 19-by-15-in [48-by-38-cm] rectangle with the long end facing you. With a rubber spatula, evenly spread the cinnamon–brown sugar mixture over the dough.

Roll the dough away from you to form a long cylinder. Cut the cylinder into fifteen 1½-in [4-cm] slices.

Take the lip from each cut piece and tuck it under the bottom of the cut side so you cover the cut side with the dough. Butter a 9-by-13-in [23-by-33-cm] baking pan. Place the rolls in the pan cut-side up, spacing them about ½ in [12 mm] apart. Cover loosely with plastic wrap and let sit at room temperature for 2 hours to proof.

To make the icing (if desired), combine the confectioners' sugar and milk together in a bowl. Using a fork, mix until creamy and there are no more dry bits of sugar.

Continued . . .

Preheat the oven to 350°F [175°C].

Brush the tops of the rolls with the remaining 50 g beaten egg and sprinkle with a little turbinado sugar (if using). Bake for 35 minutes, rotating the pan halfway through baking, until golden brown. Let cool for 10 minutes. When the brioche is still warm, brush about 1 Tbsp of the icing over each roll (if desired) and serve. Store in an airtight container and eat within 2 days.

HERITAGE DINNER ROLLS

MAKES 12 ROLLS

500 g (3½ cups) sifted heritage flour (HRW/HRS), such as Red Fife or Glenn

55 g (¼ cup) sugar

6 g (1 tsp) fine sea salt

7 g (1½ tsp) instant yeast

50 g (1 large) egg

120 g (½ cup) water

120 g (½ cup) milk

113 g (½ cup) unsalted butter, cubed, plus 56 g (¼ cup) unsalted butter, melted

This is a simple, straightforward dinner roll to serve at a holiday meal. They also make great buns for pulled pork or barbecue chicken sandwiches. The most glaring ingredient in this recipe is instant yeast! How could we do this with our focus on natural starters? Well, sometimes you're in a rush and need a dinner roll that doesn't require feeding your starter beforehand. Also, when you start adding sugar and butter to a dough, it can make a natural starter act unpredictably during baking. Since we're using instant yeast here, we do need to do a touch of kneading to get the gluten activated slightly.

In the bowl of a stand mixer fitted with the dough hook, combine the flour, sugar, salt, and yeast and mix on low speed to combine.

With the mixer running on low speed, add the egg, water, and milk. Slowly add the cubed butter, a few cubes at a time, and continue mixing for 5 minutes, or until all of the butter is incorporated.

Remove the dough from the bowl and gently knead with your hands for about 1 minute. Return the dough to the bowl, cover with plastic wrap, and let sit for 45 minutes.

Take the dough out of the bowl and divide into 12 equal balls (about 50 g each). Take each ball and place in the palm of your hand and round them on the counter to create skin tension.

Coat a 10-in [25-cm] cake pan or a 10-in [25-cm] cast-iron skillet with cooking spray. Place the balls in the pan or skillet, spacing them about ¼ in [6 mm] apart. They should fit snugly into the pan and will bake into each other; you can tear or slice them apart after baking.

Cover loosely with plastic wrap and let sit in a warmer part of your kitchen for 1 hour to proof. Don't let the plastic wrap touch the dough or it will stick when you remove it.

Preheat the oven to 350°F [175°C].

Bake for 24 minutes, rotating the pan halfway through baking, until golden brown.

Remove the rolls from the oven and brush with the melted butter while still hot.

Let cool for 10 minutes and serve warm, or cool completely, cover with plastic wrap, and serve the next day. The rolls can be frozen for up to 3 months in a resealable plastic bag or an airtight container. Rewarm frozen rolls in the oven at 350°F [175°C] for 10 minutes, brush the tops with about 1 tsp butter each while warm, and serve. Once the rolls are reheated, they are best eaten that day.

HERBED DINNER ROLLS

MAKES 12 ROLLS

DOUGH

485 g (3½ cups) sifted heritage flour (HRW/HRS), such as Red Fife or Glenn

55 g (¼ cup) sugar

6 g (1 tsp) fine sea salt

7 g (1½ tsp) instant yeast

50 g (1 large) egg

120 g (½ cup) water

120 g (½ cup) milk

113 g (½ cup) unsalted butter, cubed

2 g (1 tsp) chopped fresh rosemary

2 g (1 tsp) chopped fresh thyme

ROSEMARY BUTTER

1 rosemary sprig

56 g (¼ cup) unsalted butter

For a really easy alternative to a traditional roll, we add some herbs to the dough and brush with rosemary-infused butter. It makes for a more festive addition to the meal, especially around the fall and winter holidays. The smell of baking rosemary is also a comforting, natural fragrance for the home.

In the bowl of a stand mixer fitted with the dough hook, combine the flour, sugar, salt, and yeast and mix on low speed to combine.

With the mixer running on low speed, add the egg, water, and milk. Slowly add the cubed butter, a few cubes at a time, and continue mixing for 5 minutes, or until all of the butter is incorporated. Fold in the chopped rosemary and thyme.

Remove the dough from the bowl and gently knead with your hands for about 1 minute. Return the dough to the bowl, cover with plastic wrap, and let sit for 45 minutes.

Take the dough out of the bowl and divide into 12 equal balls (about 50 g each). Take each ball and place in the palm of your hand and round them on the counter to create skin tension.

Coat a 10-in [25-cm] cake pan or a 10-in [25-cm] cast-iron skillet with cooking spray. Place the balls in the pan or skillet, spacing them about ¼ in [6 mm] apart. They should fit snugly into the pan and will bake into each other; you can tear or slice them apart after baking.

Cover loosely with plastic wrap and let sit in a warmer part of your kitchen for 1 hour to proof. Don't let the plastic wrap

Continued . . .

touch the dough or it will stick when you remove it.

Preheat the oven to 350°F [175°C].

Bake for 24 minutes, rotating the pan halfway through baking, until golden brown.

Meanwhile, to make the rosemary butter, in a small microwavable bowl or in a small saucepan with the rosemary sprig, melt the 50 g [¼ cup] butter.

Remove the rolls from the oven and brush with the rosemary-infused melted butter while still hot.

Let cool for 10 minutes and serve warm, or cool completely, cover with plastic wrap, and serve the next day. The rolls can be frozen for up to 3 months in a resealable plastic bag or an airtight container. Rewarm frozen rolls in the oven at 350°F [175°C] for 10 minutes, brush the tops with about 1 tsp butter each while warm, and serve. Once the rolls are reheated, they are best eaten that day.

HERITAGE CORNBREAD

SERVES 8 TO 16

225 g (1½ cups) fine-milled heritage cornmeal, such as Bloody Butcher or Floriani Flint

225 g (1¾ cups) sifted heritage flour (SWS), such as White Sonora or Richland

55 g (¼ cup) sugar

2 g (1 tsp) freshly grated lemon zest

12 g (2¼ tsp) baking powder

3 g (½ tsp) fine sea salt

75 g (½ cup) starter (page 47)

150 g (about 3 large) eggs

350 g (1½ cups) buttermilk

127 g (½ cup plus 1 Tbsp) unsalted butter, melted, plus more for the pan and for serving

It was through Andy Hazzard of Hazzard Free Farm (see page 106) that I discovered the flavorful notes of heritage corn. Try to find a small farmer in your area who grows it.

This recipe calls for Bloody Butcher or Floriani Flint, which has origins in Italy. We use White Sonora wheat for this recipe because it's light and fluffy and its mild flavor doesn't overpower the corn. Using your natural bread starter helps coax out the unique flavors of the corn.

Preheat the oven to 375°F [190°C].

Combine the cornmeal, flour, sugar, lemon zest, baking powder, and salt in a large bowl.

In a separate large bowl, whisk together the starter, eggs, buttermilk, and melted butter.

Add the egg mixture to the flour mixture and stir with a wooden spoon or rubber spatula to combine.

Butter an 8-in [20-cm] square baking pan or an 8-in [20-cm] round cast-iron pan. Pour the batter into the pan.

Bake for 10 minutes. Lower the oven to 350°F [175°C] and bake for 20 minutes more, or until light gold on the top and a metal skewer or toothpick inserted into the center comes out clean.

Let cool in the pan for 5 minutes. Slice into 16 squares (or 8 triangles if using a round cast-iron pan) and serve warm with butter. Or store in an airtight container and enjoy the next day. The cornbread can be frozen for up to 2 months in a resealable plastic bag. To reheat, place the cornbread in a sealed aluminum foil pouch and bake at 325°F [160°C] for 8 to 10 minutes, or until warm.

HABANERO-CILANTRO-LIME CORNBREAD

SERVES 8 TO 16

225 g (1½ cups) fine-milled heritage cornmeal

225 g (1¾ cups) sifted heritage flour (SWS), such as White Sonora or Richland

55 g (¼ cup) sugar

2 g (1 tsp) freshly grated lemon zest

12 g (2¼ tsp) baking powder

3 g (½ tsp) fine sea salt

75 g (½ cup) starter (page 47)

150 g (about 3 large) eggs

350 g (1½ cups) buttermilk

113 g (½ cup) unsalted butter, melted, plus more for the pan

1 habanero chile, seeded and finely chopped

2 g (1 tsp) freshly grated lime zest

60 g (¼ cup) fresh lime juice

12 g (⅓ cup) chopped fresh cilantro

This cornbread packs heat. I would recommend wearing gloves when chopping the habanero chile. You can always cut the amount of habanero pepper by half if you prefer a little less heat, but then again, I'm a wimp when it comes to spicy food.

Preheat the oven to 375°F [190°C].

Combine the cornmeal, flour, sugar, lemon zest, baking powder, and salt in a large bowl.

In a separate large bowl, whisk together the starter, eggs, buttermilk, and melted butter.

Add the egg mixture to the flour mixture and stir with a wooden spoon or rubber spatula to combine. In a small bowl, mix together the chile, lime zest, lime juice, and cilantro. Gently fold the mixture into the batter.

Butter an 8-in [20-cm] square baking pan or an 8-in [20-cm] round cast-iron pan. Pour the batter into the pan.

Bake for 10 minutes. Lower the oven to 350°F [175°C] and bake for 20 minutes more, or until light gold on the top and a metal skewer or toothpick inserted into the center comes out clean.

Let cool in the pan for 5 minutes. Slice into 16 squares (or 8 triangles if using a round cast-iron pan) and serve warm with butter. Or store in an airtight container and enjoy the next day. The cornbread can be frozen for up to 2 months in a resealable plastic bag. To reheat, place the cornbread in a sealed aluminum foil pouch and bake at 325°F [160°C] for 8 to 10 minutes, or until warm.

CARAMELIZED ONION AND PARM CORNBREAD

SERVES 8 TO 16

CARAMELIZED ONION

12 g (1 Tbsp) olive oil

14 g (1 Tbsp) unsalted butter

200 g (1 medium) yellow onion, diced

BATTER

225 g (1½ cups) fine-milled heritage cornmeal

225 g (1¾ cups) sifted heritage flour (SWS), such as White Sonora or Richland

55 g (¼ cup) sugar

2 g (1 tsp) freshly grated lemon zest

12 g (2¼ tsp) baking powder

3 g (½ tsp) fine sea salt

75 g (½ cup) starter (page 47)

150 g (about 3 large) eggs

350 g (1½ cups) buttermilk

113 g (½ cup) unsalted butter, melted, plus more for the pan and for serving

90 g (1 cup) grated Parmesan cheese

The rich, caramel flavor of the onions and umami from the Parmesan brings out the distinct flavors of the heritage cornmeal we use.

To make the caramelized onion, heat the olive oil and butter in a large sauté pan over medium heat. Add the onion and cook for 15 minutes, or until tender and caramelized, stirring occasionally and lowering the heat as necessary to ensure the onions don't burn. Remove the pan from the heat and set aside to cool.

To make the batter, combine the cornmeal, flour, sugar, lemon zest, baking powder, and salt in a large bowl.

In a separate large bowl, whisk together the starter, eggs, buttermilk, and melted butter.

Add the egg mixture to the flour mixture and stir with a wooden spoon or rubber spatula to combine. Gently fold the caramelized onion and Parmesan into the dough.

Butter an 8-in [20-cm] square baking pan or an 8-in [20-cm] round cast-iron pan. Pour the batter into the pan.

Bake for 10 minutes. Lower the oven to 350°F [175°C] and bake for 20 minutes more, or until light gold on the top and a metal skewer or toothpick inserted into the center comes out clean.

Let cool in the pan for 5 minutes. Slice into 16 squares (or 8 triangles if using a round cast-iron pan) and serve warm with butter. Or store in an airtight container and enjoy the next day. The cornbread can be frozen for up to 2 months in a resealable plastic bag. To reheat, place the cornbread in a sealed aluminum foil pouch and bake at 325°F [160°C] for 8 to 10 minutes, or until warm.

NAPERVILLE BANANA BREAD

MAKES 1 LOAF

113 g (½ cup) unsalted butter, at room temperature, plus more for the pan

205 g (¾ cup) sugar

100 g (2 large) eggs

4 g (1 tsp) pure vanilla extract

300 g (2 cups) sifted heritage flour (HRW/HRS), such as Turkey Red

3 g (½ tsp) fine sea salt

2 g (½ tsp) baking soda

250 g (2 medium) very ripe bananas, mashed

120 g (⅔ cup) dark chocolate chips (optional)

70 g (½ cup) walnuts, chopped (optional)

My mom did not love to cook, but her go-to baking recipe was fruit bread. She would make large batches and freeze them so we always had something fruit-filled and a little sweet in our school lunches.

I spent most of my formative childhood years in Naperville, an old farming town turned Chicago suburb. It pretty much represented everything I disliked as a teenager: strip malls, subdivisions, and retention ponds. But this bread was a large part of my childhood there, and having moved back to the Midwest from the West Coast, I have come to appreciate many reminders of my childhood home: the massive old rock quarry we used to swim in, a bustling river, a thriving "downtown" area with historic architecture, and this delicious banana bread.

The key to this recipe is to use bananas that are almost completely black—the darker the better. The bananas become much sweeter and softer as they ripen, and as a result, will bake better. Let bananas ripen on your countertop or in a brown paper bag until they reach this stage. I prefer to use Turkey Red flour or another hard red wheat because it adds a little more structure to the bread and gives it a beautiful nutty taste that pairs well with the bananas.

Preheat the oven to 350°F [175°C]. Butter an 8-by-4-in [20-by-10-cm] loaf pan.

In the bowl of a stand mixer fitted with the paddle attachment or using a handheld mixer and a large bowl, beat the butter and sugar on medium speed until the sugar crystals have dissolved, about 3 minutes. Add the eggs and vanilla and beat until well combined.

Continued . . .

In a medium bowl, sift together the flour, salt, and baking soda and add to the butter-sugar mixture. Mix on low speed until there are no visible traces of flour. With the mixer running on low speed, add the bananas and mix until just combined.

Using a wooden spoon, fold in the chocolate chips and walnuts (if using). Pour the batter into the prepared loaf pan.

Bake for 50 minutes, or until golden brown on top and a metal skewer or toothpick inserted into the center comes out clean.

Let cool in the pan for 5 minutes, then run a knife along the edges of the pan. Carefully tip the loaf out of the pan. Cut into thick slices and serve warm or at room temperature. Banana bread can be stored in the freezer for up to 3 months in a resealable plastic bag or an airtight container. To thaw, let the bread sit on the counter, still in the plastic bag, overnight. The next day, serve the bread when it reaches room temperature.

CARROT GINGER BREAD

MAKES 1 LOAF

- 150 g (1½ cups) peeled and shredded carrots
- 2 g (1 tsp) freshly grated lemon zest
- 3 g (½ tsp) fine sea salt
- 250 g (1¾ cups) heritage whole-wheat flour (HRW/HRS), such as Turkey Red, Red Fife, or Rouge de Bordeaux
- 100 g (½ cup) lightly packed light brown sugar
- 55 g (¼ cup) granulated sugar
- 5 g (1 tsp) baking powder
- 5 g (1 tsp) baking soda
- 3 g (1 tsp) ground Ceylon cinnamon
- 40 g (¼ cup) crystallized ginger nibs
- 2 g (1 tsp) ground ginger
- 200 g (¾ cup) unsweetened applesauce
- 85 g (⅓ cup) sour cream
- 113 g (½ cup) unsalted butter, melted
- 100 g (2 large) eggs
- 70 g (½ cup) chopped walnuts (optional)

Just like freshly milled flour, we find it's just as important to use fresh spices—nothing that's been in the cupboard for more than 6 months. At Hewn, we buy small amounts of spices on a frequent basis. We are fortunate to have a great spice merchant in Evanston who keeps our supply stocked. Once you realize the difference in freshness and taste, it will be hard to go back to the old grocery store stuff, just like with flour. We use crystallized ginger nibs and they add a great kick and chew to this bread, so we highly recommend trying to track them down, but it's OK to omit them.

Preheat the oven to 375°F [190°C]. Butter a 9-by-5-in [23-by-12-cm] loaf pan.

In a large bowl, toss the carrots with the lemon zest and salt. Set aside.

In a medium bowl, whisk together the flour, brown sugar, granulated sugar, baking powder, baking soda, cinnamon, ginger nibs, and ground ginger.

In a colander placed over the sink, use your hands to squeeze out as much liquid as possible from the carrot mixture. Return the carrot mixture to the large bowl, then add the applesauce, sour cream, melted butter, and eggs and stir until just combined. Add the flour mixture to the carrot mixture and fold until combined.

Using a wooden spoon, fold in the walnuts (if using). Pour the batter into the prepared loaf pan.

Bake for 10 minutes. Lower the oven to 350°F [175°C] and bake for 40 minutes more, or until a metal skewer or toothpick inserted into the center comes out clean.

Let cool in the pan for 5 minutes, then run a knife along the edges of the pan. Carefully tip the loaf out of the pan. Cut into thick slices and serve warm or at room temperature. Carrot ginger bread can be stored in the freezer for up to 3 months in a resealable plastic bag or an airtight container. To thaw, let the bread sit on the counter, still in the plastic bag, overnight. The next day, serve the bread when it reaches room temperature.

CHAPTER FOUR

MUFFINS AND SCONES

MORNING GLORY MUFFINS

MAKES 12 MUFFINS

200 g (2 or 3) raw carrots, peeled

122 g (1 medium) apple or ripe pear, peeled

65 g (⅓ cup) lightly packed light brown sugar

40 g (⅓ cup) chopped walnuts

75 g (½ cup) golden raisins, soaked in hot water, drained

70 g (½ cup) sunflower seeds

40 g (¼ cup) flaxseeds

6 g (2 tsp) ground Ceylon cinnamon

1 g (½ tsp) ground ginger

3 g (½ tsp) fine sea salt

10 g (2 tsp) baking soda

150 g (3 large) eggs

140 g (⅔ cup) grapeseed oil

8 g (2 tsp) pure vanilla extract or paste

253 g (1¾ cups) sifted heritage flour (HRW/HRS), such as Red Fife or Marquis

25 g (¼ cup) stone-rolled heritage oats

A customer once asked us if we had a "healthy" muffin with fruit and seeds, so we worked to come up with one that's packed with whole grains and fruit, yet still light and delicious. Timmy, one of our pastry chefs, created this now-favorite muffin at the bakery. Some days we sell out of them before we finish even filling the display case. The sweetness from the fresh and dried fruit balance out the earthy, whole-wheat taste of the Turkey Red flour.

Preheat the oven to 350°F [175°C]. Butter a 12-cup muffin pan.

Grate the carrots and apple (or pear) using a box grater and add the shredded fruit to a large bowl. Add the brown sugar and toss well. Stir in the walnuts, raisins, sunflower seeds, flaxseeds, cinnamon, ginger, salt, and baking soda until well combined.

In a small bowl, whisk together the eggs, grapeseed oil, and vanilla until well combined. Add to the carrot-apple mixture and mix until combined. Fold in the flour just until there are no visible traces of flour. Do not overmix.

Using an ice cream scoop, spoon the batter evenly among the prepared muffin cups; the cups should be three-quarters full. Sprinkle with the oats.

Bake for 22 to 23 minutes, or until a metal skewer or toothpick inserted into the center comes out clean. Let cool in the pan for 5 minutes. Serve warm or at room temperature, or freeze in a resealable plastic bag for up to 3 months. To reheat, set on the counter until thawed and warm in a 325°F [160°C] oven for 10 minutes.

HERITAGE CORN AND BERRY MUFFINS

MAKES 12 MUFFINS

BATTER

135 g (⅔ cup) granulated sugar

100 g (2 large) eggs, lightly beaten

100 g (½ cup) heavy cream

85 g (⅓ cup) sour cream

8 g (2 tsp) pure vanilla extract

56 g (¼ cup) unsalted butter, melted

253 g (1¾ cups) sifted heritage flour (SWS), such as White Sonora or Richland

75 g (½ cup) fine-milled Floriani Flint or other heritage cornmeal

7 g (1½ tsp) baking powder

7 g (1½ tsp) baking soda

3 g (½ tsp) fine sea salt

125 g (1 cup) strawberries, quartered, or blueberries

STREUSEL TOPPING

45 g (¼ cup) lightly packed brown sugar

50 g (½ cup) stone-rolled heritage oats

15 g (1 Tbsp) unsalted butter, at room temperature

At Hewn, we have access to such interesting cornmeal varieties that we try to add it into as many recipes as we can. For this recipe, we like to use Floriani Flint corn. Floriani Flint is an heirloom variety from the Italian Alps, but it also grows well in Illinois. It has a very hard exterior and a nutty, smooth flavor. We like it in this muffin recipe because it adds a fuller, more savory taste and a more toothsome, slight crunchiness to the texture. The flavor of flint corn is rich and pronounced. If you can't find Floriani, any flint corn variety from your region will work well for this recipe.

Preheat the oven to 350°F [175°C]. Butter a 12-cup muffin pan.

To make the batter, stir together the granulated sugar and eggs in a large bowl until combined. Stir in the heavy cream, sour cream, and vanilla, followed by the melted butter. In a medium bowl, stir together the flour, cornmeal, baking powder, baking soda, and salt. Add the flour mixture to the egg mixture and stir just until combined. Using a wooden spoon, very gently fold in the berries. Do not overmix.

Using an ice cream scoop, spoon the batter evenly among the prepared muffin cups; the cups should be three-quarters full.

To make the streusel topping, combine the brown sugar, oats, and butter in a small bowl. Using a spoon or your hands, stir until the mixture becomes crumbly. Sprinkle about 1 Tbsp of the topping over each muffin.

Bake for 25 minutes, or until a metal skewer or toothpick inserted into the center comes out clean. Let cool in the pan for 5 minutes. Serve warm or at room temperature, or freeze in a resealable plastic bag for up to 3 months. To reheat, set on the counter until thawed and warm in a 325°F [160°C] oven for 10 minutes.

JOHN AND HALEE WEPKING

MEADOWLARK ORGANICS, RIDGEWAY, WISCONSIN

by Amelia Levin

HALEE WEPKING NEVER IMAGINED going from a line cook at Gabrielle Hamilton's acclaimed Prune restaurant in New York to co-farming an organic small grains farm in the middle of Wisconsin. It was at Prune that Halee met co-worker John Wepking. Lunch dates turned into real dates and, eventually, marriage. Looking for a change of scenery and lifestyle, the duo left New York for the countryside in 2014 and started a family just as they were learning the ropes of organic farming. Now, as operators of the 800-acre Meadowlark Organics, they farm various types of heritage and ancient grains that both chefs and consumers crave, and that Ellen and other bakers source for delicious, nutritious flour.

Travel to Wisconsin's Driftless Region, about 40 miles west of Madison, and it's easy to imagine the transition from big city to big nature. Untouched by melting glaciers centuries ago, the region's rolling hills not only lend charm and beauty to the area, but also functionality; many farmers are able to grow a wide variety of crops, depending on whether they're on a peak or in a valley, and animals like grazing on the lush grasses throughout. Wake up in the morning in the valley come late summer and you'll see the dewy frost on the tips of plants and crops, like a delicate dusting of snowflakes. By the end of the day, though, the sun-drenched rows soak up the rays wholeheartedly. It's this rise and fall of temperatures that make the Wepkings' hearty wheats and grains so rich and earthy.

The Wepkings were lucky enough to land the farm via Craigslist of all sources, where veteran farmer Paul Bickford of Bickford Farms had posted an ad looking for newer-generation farmers to grow organics for him, and perhaps eventually take over as he neared his retirement.

"Paul's farm was still smoldering after a huge fire when we got there," says Halee. A lightning strike on the hay shed had burned down the entire structure as well as an old dairy parlor. The timing was ripe for the help he sought. John went straight to work just a month before the couple's son was born.

That fall, after making inroads setting up crop rotation and marketing and strategic planning initiatives for Meadowlark, John had heard of other farmers in the Midwest and elsewhere growing small grains and convinced Paul to plant a few rows. He started with oats and a few different varieties of wheat, including heritage varieties like Turkey Red and Red Fife, and spelt.

"We bake with the grains ourselves all the time, since we're both avid bakers and did a fair amount of pastry while at Prune," says Halee.

While the small grains they grow are healthier, without the use of pesticides or other chemicals, the main reason for growing them

is taste. "Just like wine, you can experience the terroir of our grains," says Halee. "There are so many different flavor profiles depending on the type of grain and growing season in our area." Some wheats, like Turkey Red, can have a cinnamon taste. Others have earthier undertones. Now, the Wepkings have been able to figure out which types of wheat and small grains grow in their immediate surroundings, with their immediate climate.

Red Fife seems to be doing best, after the couple purchased a handful of seeds from Cornell University and started with 18 acres in the spring. They have also experimented with emmer, an ancient wheat, purchased from a farmer in Minnesota, as a replacement for durum in pasta making.

Most recently, they are working on building their own mill to be able to eventually not only harvest but also clean wheat berries and produce their own flour. They're hoping their production of spelt flour might set them apart because of the extra step of hulling the berries, something not many farmers want to do. Outside of wheat, the Wepkings also grow open-pollinated flint corn for polenta as well as heritage varieties of red, blue, white, and yellow corn for stone-grinding into polenta.

While John remains the forever farmer, Halee continues to straddle the line between farmer and writer. "For me, organic farming is freedom: freedom to choose the way we farm," John has written on his blog. "In a conventional system, nearly everything is prescribed for you: when and what to plant, when to spray, what to spray, where to sell your grain, how much your grain is worth. You may decide to use cover crops or no-till equipment, but beyond that, conventional grain farming is relatively devoid of choice and full of expenses that we in the organic world do not rely on to the same degree. In order to succeed, we need to listen to the world around us. Nature has no shareholders, needs no profits. Given the choice of listening to nature or listening to the businesses that exist, fundamentally, to make ever-increasing profits off of farmers, I'll listen to nature every time."

As organic farmers, the Wepkings do not spray on nitrogen, so they grow with alfalfa and other legumes. To control pests and soilborne pathogens, they stretch out their rotation with a diversity of crops and cover crops. Being in a relatively wet region, they must grow their small grain crops (including wheat) after a non-grass crop to limit the incidence of Fusarium head blight, which produces a toxin that can disqualify a crop of wheat from food-grade use. So they grow their winter wheat after alfalfa and before corn, relying on a clover and tillage radish cover crop. They are currently working on growing more rye and buckwheat in place of soybeans.

"Growing your own food is something that was really exciting to me, and also as a dancer, I enjoy the physical nature of it and feeling like what you did day to day really made a difference in life," Halee says.

Says John, "Growing wheat is not super sexy but I think it's a great life and I wish more young farmers were interested in this type of farming." Well, Ellen and the other bakers, consumers, and artisans who buy their grains think so, too.

LAVENDER LEMON MUFFINS

MAKES 12 MUFFINS

MUFFINS

135 g (⅔ cup) granulated sugar

100 g (2 large) eggs, lightly beaten

200 g (scant 1 cup) buttermilk

30 g (2 Tbsp) fresh lemon juice

8 g (2 tsp) pure vanilla extract

56 g (¼ cup) unsalted butter, melted

½ g (1 tsp) dried lavender

250 g (1¾ cups) sifted heritage flour (SWS/SRS), such as White Sonora, Richland, or Warthog

6 g (1 Tbsp) freshly grated lemon zest

7 g (1½ tsp) baking powder

5 g (1 tsp) baking soda

3 g (½ tsp) fine sea salt

STREUSEL TOPPING

45 g (¼ cup) lightly packed brown sugar

3 g (1½ tsp) freshly grated lemon zest

14 g (1 Tbsp) unsalted butter, at room temperature

I have always loved lavender—the soap, the flowers, the color, the natural cleansing properties, and of course, the refreshing scent. One day I was at our local spice house when I got a whiff of dried culinary lavender and wanted to figure out a way to use it.

Pairing it with lemon gives these muffins a bright taste and floral aroma, and the mild wheat flavors of a sifted Glenn or Red Fife flour balances everything out. When looking for lavender in a local spice shop or online, make sure to source lavender meant for cooking, not for decoration.

Preheat the oven to 350°F [175°C]. Butter a 12-cup muffin pan.

To make the batter, stir together the granulated sugar and eggs in a large bowl until combined. Stir in the buttermilk, lemon juice, and vanilla, followed by the melted butter and lavender. In a medium bowl, stir together the flour, lemon zest, baking powder, baking soda, and salt. Add the flour mixture to the egg mixture and stir just until combined.

Using an ice cream scoop, spoon the batter evenly among the prepared muffin cups; the cups should be three-quarters full.

To make the streusel topping, combine the brown sugar, lemon zest, and butter in a small bowl. Using a spoon or your hands, stir until the mixture becomes crumbly. Sprinkle about 1 Tbsp of the topping over each muffin.

Bake for 25 minutes, or until a metal skewer or toothpick inserted into the center comes out clean. Let cool in the pan for 5 minutes. Serve warm or at room temperature, or freeze in a resealable plastic bag up to 3 months. To reheat, set on the counter until thawed and warm in a 325°F [160°C] oven for 10 minutes.

BACON PARMESAN SCONES

MAKES 12 SCONES

230 g (8 oz) thick-cut sliced bacon

680 g (5 cups) sifted heritage flour (HRW/HRS), such as Rouge de Bordeaux

15 g (1 Tbsp) baking powder

5 g (1 tsp) baking soda

10 g (1½ tsp) fine sea salt

255 g (1 cup, plus 2 Tbsp) unsalted butter, cubed

400 g (1¾ cups) buttermilk

35 g (2 Tbsp) pure maple syrup

135 g (1½ cups) grated Parmesan cheese

75 g (¼ cup) ramps, chopped, or 10 g (⅓ cup) chives, chopped (optional)

We don't work with a lot of meat at the bakery, but before we had these scones, we constantly had customers asking for something with bacon in it. When making these at home, I recommend going to your local butcher for thick-cut bacon. If you really want to indulge, save the rendered bacon grease in the refrigerator and fry the scones in a little bit of it the next day to crisp up the exterior. In the spring, we like to add some local ramps to the dough; you could also add chopped fresh chives for a little kick. The Rouge de Bordeaux flour adds an earthy, peppery flavor that balances out the salt and fat from the bacon.

Preheat the oven to 350°F [175°C].

Arrange the bacon on a wire rack set on top of a rimmed baking sheet. Bake for 15 minutes, or until the bacon is crispy. Remove from the oven and let cool.

When the bacon cools to the touch, chop it into bits; you should end up with about 1½ cups chopped bits. Set aside.

In the bowl of a stand mixer fitted with the paddle attachment, combine the flour, baking powder, baking soda, and salt and mix on low speed until just combined. With the mixer running, slowly add the butter, a few cubes at a time, and mix until the butter is the size of small peas. Do not overmix. The dough should look like wet, shaggy sand.

Add the buttermilk, maple syrup, Parmesan, chopped bacon, and ramps (if using) and lightly mix with your hands until just combined.

Continued . . .

Butter a large rimmed baking sheet. Transfer the dough to a lightly floured surface and shape into a 10-by-8-in [25-by-20-cm] rectangle that's about 1 to 1½ in [2.5 to 4 cm] thick.

Using a large knife, cut the dough into twelve 2½-in [6-cm] squares. Arrange the scones on the prepared baking sheet, spacing them about 2 in [5 cm] apart.

Bake the scones for 25 to 26 minutes, or until golden around the edges and a metal skewer or toothpick inserted into the center of a scone comes out clean.

Serve warm with butter, or let cool and freeze for up to 2 months in a resealable plastic bag. To freeze unbaked scones, place the cut scones on a baking sheet and freeze until firm, then transfer to a resealable plastic bag to freeze. Pull them out as needed to bake and increase the baking time by 7 to 8 minutes.

SOURDOUGH GINGER-PEACH SCONES

MAKES 12 SCONES

435 g (3 cups) sifted heritage flour (SWS), such as White Sonora

125 g (½ cup plus 1 Tbsp) sugar

40 g (1/4 cup) crystallized ginger nibs (optional)

6 g (1 Tbsp) freshly grated lime zest

7 g (1½ tsp) baking powder

2 g (½ tsp) baking soda

3 g (½ tsp) fine sea salt

227 g (1 cup) cold unsalted butter, cubed

100 g (1 cup) starter (page 47)

50 g (¼ cup) cold heavy cream

50 g (1 large) egg

15 g (1 Tbsp) grated fresh ginger

4 g (1 tsp) pure vanilla paste or extract

1 ripe peach, pitted and diced

Combining freshly milled heritage flour with a natural starter helps creates a really tender, moist, and tangy crumb for these scones, unlike the dry, cough-inducing scones you might be used to eating. We add baking powder and baking soda to lighten up the dough even more because this recipe doesn't have a long fermentation. Some of our customers who hail from England tell us they don't believe this is really a scone because it is too soft and buttery, so we nicknamed this our American scone. This is a great scone for the summer, when peaches are at the peak of their season. We use crystallized ginger nibs here, as we do in our Carrot Ginger Bread (page 160), but if you can't find them, just omit.

Preheat the oven to 350°F [175°C]. Butter a large rimmed baking sheet.

In the bowl of a stand mixer fitted with the paddle attachment, combine the flour, 125 g [½ cup] of the sugar, the ginger nibs (if using), lime zest, baking powder, baking soda, and salt and mix on low speed until just combined. With the mixer running, slowly add the butter, a few cubes at a time, and mix for 1 to 2 minutes, or until the butter is the size of small peas. Do not overmix. The dough should look like wet, shaggy sand.

In a separate bowl, whisk together the starter, cream, egg, grated ginger, and vanilla. In another separate bowl, toss the peach with remaining 1 Tbsp sugar. Let stand for 5 minutes.

Slowly pour the cream mixture into the flour-butter mixture and mix on low speed until the dry ingredients are just moistened, about 45 seconds. Remove the bowl from the mixer and fold in the peach mixture with a rubber spatula.

Continued . . .

Transfer the dough to a lightly floured surface and shape into a 10-by-8-in [25-by-20-cm] rectangle that's about 1 to 11/2 in [2.5 to 4 cm] thick.

Using a large knife, cut the dough into twelve 2½-in [6-cm] squares. Arrange the scones on the prepared baking sheet, spacing them about 2 in [5 cm] apart.

Bake the scones for 18 to 20 minutes, or until golden around the edges and a metal skewer or toothpick inserted into the center of a scone comes out clean.

Serve warm with butter, or let cool and freeze for up to 2 months in a resealable plastic bag. To freeze unbaked scones, place the cut scones on a baking sheet and freeze until firm, then transfer to a resealable plastic bag to freeze. Pull them out as needed to bake and increase the baking time by 7 to 8 minutes.

SOURDOUGH MAPLE-OAT SCONES

MAKES 12 SCONES

435 g (3 cups) heritage whole-wheat flour (HRW/HRS), such as Rouge de Bordeaux

300 g (3 cups) stone-rolled heritage oats

15 g (1 Tbsp) baking powder

2 g (½ tsp) baking soda

15 g (1 Tbsp) granulated sugar

6 g (1 tsp) fine sea salt

227 g (1 cup) cold unsalted butter, cubed

100 g (scant ½ cup) buttermilk

100 g (1 cup) starter (page 47)

290 g (1 cup) pure maple syrup

100 g (2 large) eggs

4 g (1 tsp) pure vanilla extract or paste

3 g (1 tsp) ground Ceylon cinnamon

100 g (1 cup) toasted sliced almonds

125 g (¾ cup) currants

ICING (OPTIONAL)

40 g (3 Tbsp) confectioners' sugar

40 g (2 Tbsp) maple syrup

Finding the freshest old-fashioned stone-rolled oats is the key to keeping these scones light and delicious rather than heavy and dry. We use a flaky and creamy hull-less variety grown in northwest Illinois. Non-commodity oats have a wide range of flavors, and the fresher they are, the more distinct their taste. If you can't find local stone-rolled oats, you can use old-fashioned oats, just add 50 g [¼ cup] more buttermilk. Also, we love using different local maple syrups for this recipe.

Preheat the oven to 350°F [175°C]. Line a large rimmed baking sheet with parchment paper.

In the bowl of a stand mixer with the paddle attachment, combine the flour, oats, baking powder, baking soda, granulated sugar, and salt and mix on low speed just until combined.

With the mixer running, slowly add the butter, a few cubes at a time, and mix until combined, or until the butter is the size of small peas. Add the buttermilk, starter, maple syrup, eggs, vanilla, and cinnamon and mix until the dough just comes together. Do not overmix. The dough will be sticky.

Remove the bowl from the mixer and fold in the almonds and currants with a rubber spatula.

Using an ice cream scoop, spoon the dough onto the prepared baking sheet, spacing the balls about 2 in [5 cm] apart.

Bake for 18 minutes, or until light golden brown, rotating the baking sheet halfway through baking. Let cool on the baking sheet for 5 minutes.

For the icing, if using, in a small bowl, whisk the confectioners' sugar and maple syrup until smooth.

Drizzle the icing over the scones and serve warm. Store in an airtight container at room temperature for up to 2 days or freeze for up to 3 months. To reheat, set on the counter for 1 hour and then warm in a 325°F [160°C] oven for 7 to 8 minutes.

To freeze unbaked scones, place the dough balls on a baking sheet and freeze until firm, then transfer to a resealable plastic bag to freeze longer. Pull them out as needed to bake and increase the baking time by 10 minutes.

CHAPTER FIVE

CAKES, COOKIES, AND BROWNIES

SOURDOUGH TART CHERRY COFFEE CAKE

SERVES 12

This is a secret favorite at the bakery. We make only two pans of it a week and it sells out before 10 a.m. At home, this is a great way to make more use out of your bread starter, which adds a deliciously tangy note to the cake, especially when topped with a little yogurt or crème fraîche. Note you can substitute your favorite seasonal fruit for cherries.

CHERRY FILLING

250 g (2 cups) fresh or thawed frozen tart pitted cherries

110 g (½ cup) granulated sugar

20 g (2 Tbsp) cornstarch

15 g (1 Tbsp) fresh lemon juice

4 g (1 tsp) pure vanilla extract

DOUGH

220 g (1½ cups) sifted heritage flour (SWS), such as White Sonora or Richland

75 g (⅓ cup) granulated sugar

2 g (½ tsp) baking powder

2 g (½ tsp) baking soda

3 g (½ tsp) fine sea salt

113 g (½ cup) unsalted butter

150 g (1½ cups) starter (page 47)

50 g (1 large) egg

50 g (scant ¼ cup) buttermilk

4 g (1 tsp) pure vanilla extract

To make the filling, combine the cherries, granulated sugar, cornstarch, lemon juice, and vanilla in a heavy-bottomed saucepan. Cook over low heat for 6 to 8 minutes, stirring occasionally to prevent burning, until the mixture starts bubbling. Cook for 3 minutes longer, continuing to stir, until the mixture thickens. If the mixture thickens too much, stir in 15 to 30 g [1 to 2 Tbsp] water to thin it out. Remove from the heat and let cool while preparing the dough.

Preheat the oven to 325°F [160°C].

To make the dough, combine the flour, granulated sugar, baking powder, baking soda, and salt in a medium bowl. Cut in the butter using a pastry blender or two knives until the butter is the size of small peas.

In a separate bowl, whisk together the starter, egg, buttermilk, and vanilla, then add to the flour-butter mixture and stir until the dry ingredients are just moistened.

Butter a 9-by-13-in [23-by-33-cm] baking pan. Transfer half of the dough to the pan, using a spatula to spread it into an even layer. Spread the cherry filling over the dough. Use an ice cream scooper to drop small balls of the remaining dough over the fruit, spaced about 2 in [5 cm] apart.

Continued . . .

STREUSEL TOPPING

50 g (½ cup) stone-rolled heritage oats

45 g (¼ cup) packed light brown sugar

30 g (¼ cup) chopped almonds, pecans, or walnuts

3 g (½ tsp) fine sea salt

For the streusel topping, combine the oats, brown sugar, nuts, and salt in a small bowl. Using a spoon or your hands, stir until the mixture becomes crumbly. Sprinkle over the top layer of dough.

Bake for 45 minutes, or until a metal skewer or toothpick inserted into the center comes out clean. Let stand for 20 minutes. Serve warm.

LEMON POUND CAKE

SERVES 8

BATTER

226 g (1 cup) unsalted butter, at room temperature

295 g (1⅓ cups) sugar

6 g (1 Tbsp) freshly grated lemon zest

200 g (4 large) eggs

290 g (2 cups) sifted heritage flour (HRS/HRW), such as Rouge de Bordeaux

2 g (½ tsp) baking powder

6 g (1 tsp) fine sea salt

65 g (¼ cup) crème fraîche

SOAKER

55 g (¼ cup) sugar

53 g (¼ cup) water

115 g (½ cup) fresh lemon juice

When we first opened the bakery, my brother's fiancée, who is from France, told us that we needed some sliced sweet cakes. She took a few minutes to describe what she meant, and we all looked at her very confused. Then one of our employees noted she was talking about pound cake. It was a perfect suggestion, so we went to work right away on developing a recipe using Rouge de Bordeaux flour. The delicate wheat adds another depth of flavor to the cake beyond just butter, sugar, and lemon.

Preheat the oven to 350°F [175°C]. Butter and flour an 8-by-4-in [20-by-10-cm] loaf pan.

To make the batter, in the bowl of a stand mixer fitted with the paddle attachment or using a handheld mixer and a large bowl, beat the butter and sugar together on medium speed until the sugar crystals have dissolved, about 2 minutes. Add the lemon zest and eggs and beat on low speed until well combined.

In a medium bowl, stir together the flour, baking powder, and salt and add to the butter-sugar mixture. Mix on low speed until there are no visible traces of flour. Add the crème fraîche and mix on low speed until just combined

Spoon the batter into the prepared loaf pan. Bake for 15 minutes. Remove from the oven and use a sharp knife to cut a slit down the middle. This will allow the pound cake to open up slightly.

Return to the oven, reduce the heat to 325°F [160°C], and bake for 45 minutes more, or until a metal skewer or toothpick inserted into the center comes out clean.

Continued . . .

Meanwhile, to make the lemon soaker, combine the sugar and water in a small saucepan and bring to a boil. Remove from the heat, stir in the lemon juice, and set aside to cool.

Remove the cake from the oven and let cool in the pan for 30 minutes. Once cool, run a knife along the edges of the pan and carefully tip the loaf out of the pan and onto a wire rack set over a rimmed baking sheet. Using a skewer, poke 4 or 5 holes on each side, top and bottom of the cake. This will allow the soaker to be absorbed into the interior of the loaf. Spoon the lemon soaker over the top and along the sides and bottom of the pound cake.

To add icing as pictured, follow the method on page 180.

Cut the cake into thick slices and serve. Or cover tightly in plastic wrap and store at room temperature for up to 4 days.

HAROLD WILKEN

JANIE'S FARM

by Amelia Levin

WHEN HIS SON, ROSS, first expressed interest in milling, fifth-generation farmer Harold Wilken and his wife, Sandy, knew they didn't want to expose their children to the same pesticides and insecticides Harold had ingested since he was a young child working on his family's conventional farm in Iroquois County, Illinois.

"I don't care what happens to me at this point, but I won't let my kids get near the stuff," says Harold, who suffered migraines and other side effects of inhaling the chemical fumes. He has a slightly hoarse voice and scars from his salivary gland cancer surgery in 2008 that are still visible on his neck. They are a regular reminder that years of exposure to pesticides, insecticides, and other modern agriculture chemicals were likely the culprit.

Thoughts of going 100 percent organic first started to simmer when his daughter Janie was killed in a car accident in 2001 at the young age of fifteen. Harold's life was changed forever and not just in the obviously tragic way. Janie knew how passionate Harold was about organics. Soon after she died, a neighboring organic farmer, Herman Brockman, asked if he wanted to farm some crop for him. It took a spiritual connection to his loss—and some time to grieve—to find that motivation to do in 2005 what Janie had always wanted him to do. It was then that Harold's farm became certified organic and the long transition process began.

Harold had other hurdles when going organic; several farm neighbors looked at him sideways when he talked of his plans, with one even saying to him, "If you're not independently wealthy, don't do it." Turns out, however, that organic grains are actually profitable, not to mention that he now has a growing network of supportive, like-minded farmers. He's even become a mentor to others choosing the same path.

Today, most of the 2,370 acres are USDA certified organic, with just a handful of acres still in transition, thanks in part to the hard work from Harold's nephew, Tim Vaske. It takes years just to detox the land and—literally—weed out all the chemicals in order to make the soil healthy again.

"I call myself a recovering conventional farmer," Harold says as we take the dusty pickup truck backroading out to the wheat fields. On the outskirts of the long rows of both hard spring and hard winter heritage Warthog, Glenn, and Turkey Red wheat, you'll see some organic corn and popcorn, oats, pumpkins, black beans, alfalfa, and soybeans, though not the conventional kind. The latter he sells to a local organic tofu producer, Phoenix Bean.

"You like tofu?" I ask Harold, whose tall, football-like stance and tanned, weathered skin looks nothing like that of a lanky vegan from the city.

"You would be surprised," he says, flashing his smile. "I love the teriyaki-marinated kind the best."

I get out, instantly kicking myself for not wearing jeans even on this hot day. The feather-shaped tops of the stalks scratch our legs as we gently navigate the field. Harold reassures us that this particular wheat—Warthog—is a hardy winter wheat, the kind that's planted in the fall and harvested in the spring. It's used to being "knocked down" a little by the elements. At the foot of the stalks we see red clover, the nitrogen-rich cover crop meant to keep the soil healthy and strong.

He reaches down to strip away some of the wheat berries off a tawny, sun-dried stalk of Turkey Red, rolling them together between his callused fingers. He hands us the little berries left behind like peanuts in their cracked shells. We crunch down on a few at once, noting the toasted almond flavor. When we pass by the Glenn, he does the same for us. It's much milder, sweeter, and creamy in flavor, almost like a lightly buttered popcorn.

Later, we check out the 20-foot-high, fully automated, Bluetooth-powered, temperature- and humidity-controlled grain bins he sourced and put together himself. He did this because the alternative was to send the wheat to one of the many huge commodity-grain elevators. There, it would have been mixed with other wheat berries and no one would know if the flour came from his wheat. After drying out the wheat berries further with fans to bring heat and humidity levels down, they will be loaded by machine-powered conveyors into the back of trucks. The crop is then hauled to buyers like Journeyman Distillery, or back to Harold's mill, 3 miles up the road in Ashkum.

It's there that Ross and mill manager Jill Brockman, who grew up and worked on her family's organic farm, mill the wheat in batches as soon as Ellen and other bakers and shops place their orders. They have a few bags of freshly milled wheat that can sit for 2 days tops, so the team prefers to store the berries and then mill them to order. It was through Jill's sister, Tara, another Evanston resident and Hewn regular, that Ellen came to find out about Harold and his fresh flour.

Jill shows me the milling system, which Ross, a smart and savvy recent University of Illinois graduate, put together after purchasing the stone mill from a century-old maker in Denmark, along with other parts from millers in Seattle.

We climb up the steps to the horizontal "pod," which is about 5 feet wide, with three compartments: an opening at the top to take in the dried and cleaned wheat, a middle where the stones grind against each other to pulverize, and a third fitted with special screens that sift out (or don't sift) the germ and bran depending on the extraction rate that Jill selects, before going into the hopper. The higher the extraction rate, the more the germ and bran is left intact, making it a stronger whole-wheat flour that's best for breads. The lower the extraction rate, the lighter the flour becomes, making it more suitable for pastries.

It's part art, part science, she says. The defined muscles in her slender arms also suggest milling is part workout—the 50-pound bags of wheat berries need to be lifted and poured into the mill. Jill stores the fresh flour before it is delivered or picked up in a temperature-controlled warehouse to protect the natural—and healthy—enzymes in the grain from too much heat or humidity. Even dealing with so much flour, there's not a dust particle to be seen in the entire 3,000-square-foot space.

Back in the office, Ellen, Harold, Ross, and Jill brainstorm potential packaging labels and marketing names for the different flours, from high-extraction whole-wheat varieties to more sifted, softer flours similar to all-purpose and pastry flour, as they gear up for some retail sales on the horizon. It was Ellen who suggested they look to the different Chicago-area river branches, like Calumet, Rock, Chicago, Mackinaw, Iroquois, and Des Plaines, to distinguish the different types.

Ellen prefers Harold's higher-extraction Glenn, Calumet, Rock, and Turkey Red (Mackinaw) wheat flours for bread; his milder-flavored, all-purpose–style Warthog (Iroquois, with 85 percent extraction) for scones, brioche, and biscotti; and finer-sifted Glenn (Chicago, with 70 percent extraction) for other lighter baked goods. The organic Erisman, a soft red winter wheat, is being milled for pastry flour (Des Plaines, with 70 percent extraction). It took working with bakers like Ellen and doing some baking themselves for Harold and his team to figure out which wheat was better suited for breads or other baked goods.

The rivers make for a fitting naming system, given the history of heritage wheat in this region. Before the commoditization and the building of the railroad system in Chicago, grain farmers packed up their wheat berries in sacks and shipped them downstream to the city on river barges (see page 26).

We're nearing the midafternoon and Ross is getting antsy. He checks his trusty handheld device sending him the humidity level of the field to determine if the wheat's dry enough to harvest yet. The farm just came off a week's worth of heavy rain and storms, so he's nervous, though his gentle demeanor hides it. "Too wet—not ready yet," Harold says. There might not be any wheat harvested that day. Had they gone the conventional wheat-growing route, they would have already sprayed their crop with glyphosate 2 weeks earlier to dry everything out without the need for dry air, wind, and sun.

And so it goes with sensitive, heritage wheat farming in the United States, even today, with modern equipment and technology. Growing chemical-free heritage wheat requires farmers to rely on age-old techniques and intuitions. Even over time, some things never change.

BUCKWHEAT HONEY MADELEINES

MAKES 12 MADELEINES

BATTER

200 g (¾ cup plus 2 Tbsp) unsalted butter, plus more for the pan

200 g (4 large) eggs

150 g (⅔ cup) sugar

40 g (3 Tbsp) honey, preferably buckwheat

195 g (1⅓ cups) sifted heritage flour (SWS), such as White Sonora or Richland, plus more for the pan

7 g (1½ tsp) baking powder

3 g (½ tsp) fine sea salt

2 g (1 tsp) freshly grated orange zest

SOAKER

60 g (⅓ cup) buckwheat honey

60 g (¼ cup) lukewarm water

We love madeleines at Hewn. They are the perfect size for a little afternoon treat and they are really easy to make. After attending a honey summit last year, Spencer came back with a burning desire to find more uses for the staple. He discovered a dark local honey collected from the nectar of buckwheat flowers, which really shows through in this recipe, but any good-quality raw local honey will do. Note that you will need a madeleine pan for this classic recipe. Also, this batter needs to chill overnight for the best results.

To make the batter, melt the butter in a small saucepan over medium heat and continue to cook until the butter takes on a light brown color, watching closely so it doesn't burn, 2 to 3 minutes. Strain the butter through a fine-mesh sieve set over a bowl and let cool to room temperature.

In the bowl of a stand mixer fitted with the whisk attachment, beat the eggs and sugar together on high speed until light and fluffy and doubled in volume, about 5 minutes.

With the mixer running on low speed, slowly pour in the brown butter and continue to mix until just blended.

Remove the bowl from the mixer. With a rubber spatula, gently fold in the honey, flour, baking powder, salt, and orange zest until smooth. Cover the bowl with plastic wrap and refrigerate the batter for at least 4 hours or overnight.

Preheat the oven to 350°F [175°C]. Butter a madeleine mold with 12 wells. Sprinkle flour into each well, tapping out any excess.

Continued . . .

Fill a pastry bag with the batter or use a spoon to fill each of the greased wells with about 2 Tbsp batter. Bake for 9 to 10 minutes, or until there is a tall peak on the top of each madeleine and it is golden brown.

Remove from the oven and immediately invert the madeleines onto a wire rack. Let the madeleines cool completely, about 30 minutes.

Meanwhile, to make the soaker, combine the honey and water in a small saucepan and cook over medium-high heat, stirring occasionally, until the honey dissolves, about 3 minutes. Set aside to cool slightly, about 10 minutes.

Brush each madeleine with the honey syrup and serve. The madeleines will keep in an airtight container for 2 days, or freeze in resealable plastic bags for up to 6 months.

CLASSIC CHOCOLATE CHIP COOKIES

MAKES 15 COOKIES

212 g (1 cup) unsalted butter, at room temperature

150 g (⅔ cup) granulated sugar

165 g (¾ cup plus 1 Tbsp) lightly packed brown sugar

100 g (2 large) eggs

4 g (1 tsp) pure vanilla paste or extract

338 g (2⅓ cups) sifted heritage flour (HRW/HRS), such as Red Fife or Marquis

6 g (1 tsp) fine sea salt

2 g (½ tsp) baking soda

230 g (1¼ cups) dark chocolate chips

Our chocolate chip cookies are my family's favorite Hewn item, besides the bread, of course! While this is a very straightforward, classic cookie recipe, using freshly milled heritage flour makes them taste so much richer and complex. You can actually taste the nuance of the wheat coming through the cookie, not just straight butter and sugar. Pairing dark chocolate with a hard red wheat works as well as a dark chocolate and a glass of pinot noir. If you are unable to find vanilla paste, buy a vanilla bean and scrape the beans out before adding to the recipe. You can also use extract, but paste or whole bean will give the cookie a purer vanilla flavor.

Preheat the oven to 325°F [160°C]. Line a large rimmed baking sheet with parchment paper.

In the bowl of a stand mixer fitted with the paddle attachment, beat the butter, granulated sugar, and brown sugar on low speed for 2 to 3 minutes, or until creamy. Do not overmix. Scrape down the bowl. With the mixer running on low speed, add the eggs, one at a time, followed by the vanilla paste, and mix until combined.

In a separate bowl, stir together the flour, salt, and baking soda, then slowly add to the butter-sugar mixture and mix until the dry ingredients are just moistened.

Scrape down the bowl again. With the mixer running on low speed, add the chocolate chips and mix for 30 to 45 seconds, just until the chips are incorporated. It is best to refrigerate the dough for at least 30 minutes before baking, as it keeps the cookies from spreading too thin, though the chilling step is optional.

Continued . . .

Using an ice cream scoop, spoon the dough onto the prepared baking sheet, spacing them 2 in [5 cm] apart.

Bake for 14 minutes, rotating the baking sheet halfway through, until golden brown. Let cool on a wire rack for 10 minutes and serve warm. Or let cool completely and store in an airtight container at room temperature for up to 5 days or freeze for up to 3 months. Just pull them frozen and thaw to enjoy. I like to pack them cold in our kids' lunch boxes. The cookies thaw by lunchtime!

GINGER COOKIES

MAKES 15 COOKIES

150 g (¾ cup) nonhydrogenated vegetable shortening

56 g (½ cup) unsalted butter, at room temperature

275 g (1½ cups) lightly packed brown sugar

100 g (2 large) eggs

120 g (⅓ cup) molasses

30 g (2 Tbsp) grated fresh ginger with juice

400 g (2¾ cups) heritage whole-wheat flour (HRW/HRS), such as Turkey Red

6 g (1¼ tsp) baking soda

6 g (2 tsp) ground Ceylon cinnamon

4 g (2 tsp) ground cloves

4 g (2 tsp) ground ginger

6 g (1 tsp) fine sea salt

I adapted this recipe from one of my favorite bakers. I met Leslie Mackie, founder of Macrina Bakery in Seattle, when I was in culinary school. Leslie is always so generous with her time and advice and she served as a sounding board for me when opening Hewn. Leslie's ginger cookies are delicious. We borrowed some of her ideas and added our own bent to the recipe. Be sure to buy nonhydrogenated shortening for this recipe. I know shortening may be shocking to see in the ingredient list, but it has a higher melting point than butter and no moisture, so it allows the cookie to spread less and stay more tender than crisp. If you don't eat all the cookies and don't want to freeze them, try crumbling them for a topping on ice cream, or fold them into a pie. I love using Turkey Red flour for this recipe because the cinnamon brings out the cinnamon notes of the wheat.

In the bowl of a stand mixer fitted with the paddle attachment, beat the shortening and butter on low speed for 2 to 3 minutes, or until creamy. Add the brown sugar and mix until well combined.

In a small bowl, stir together the eggs, molasses, and grated ginger and juice, then slowly add to the butter-shortening mixture and mix on low speed until combined.

In a medium bowl, stir together the flour, baking soda, cinnamon, cloves, ground ginger, and salt. Add the flour mixture to the butter-egg mixture and mix on low speed until there are no visible traces of flour.

Refrigerate the dough for at least 1 hour before baking, as it keeps the cookies from spreading too thin.

Preheat the oven to 350°F [175°C]. Line a large rimmed baking sheet with parchment paper.

Using an ice cream scoop, spoon the dough onto the prepared baking sheet pan, spacing them 2 in [5 cm] apart.

Bake for 12 minutes, rotating the baking sheet halfway through, until golden brown. Let cool on a wire rack for 10 minutes and serve warm or at room temperature after 45 minutes of cooling. Or let cool completely and store in an airtight container at room temperature for up to 5 days. These cookies can also be frozen for up to 2 months.

FINGERPRINT COOKIES

MAKES 12 COOKIES

227 g (1 cup) unsalted butter, at room temperature

110 g (½ cup) lightly packed brown sugar

100 g (2 large) eggs

4 g (1 tsp) pure vanilla paste or extract

290 g (2 cups) sifted heritage flour (SWS), such as White Sonora or Richland

3 g (½ tsp) fine sea salt

105 g (¾ cup) finely chopped walnuts (optional)

80 g (¼ cup) your favorite homemade or store-bought raspberry or apricot jam

These are great cookies to make with kids, who love pushing their little fingers into the dough and then filling it up the jam. In fact, this is one of my top three recipes to bake with the kids in our blended family. Use your favorite homemade or local jam. A soft white wheat gives these cookies a nice clean look and a silky flavor.

In the bowl of a stand mixer fitted with the paddle attachment, beat the butter and sugar on medium speed until light and fluffy, about 3 minutes.

With the mixer running on low speed, add the eggs, one at a time, followed by the vanilla, and mix until combined.

In a separate bowl, stir together the flour and salt, then gradually add to the butter-sugar mixture and mix on low speed until there are no visible traces of flour and the dough forms a loose ball.

Remove the dough from the bowl and shape into an 8- to 10-in- [20- to 25-cm-] long cylinder that's about 3 in [7.5 cm] in diameter.

Spread the walnuts (if using) on a work surface and roll the dough in the walnuts to coat the exterior.

OPTIONAL STEP: For a tighter log, lay a sheet of parchment paper or a silicone baking mat on a counter. Place the dough on the parchment and roll the parchment around the dough, pulling to tighten it around the log.

Keep the dough wrapped in the parchment (or wrap it if you skipped the previous optional step) and refrigerate for 1 hour before slicing.

Continued . . .

Preheat the oven to 350°F [175°C]. Line a rimmed baking sheet with parchment paper.

With a sharp knife, cut the dough log into ½-in [12-mm] slices. Arrange the slices, cut-side up, on the prepared baking sheet, spacing them 2 in [5 cm] apart.

Using your two middle fingers, make a small indentation in each cookie. Be sure to not press so hard on the dough that you cut through it. Spoon about 10 g [1 tsp] of jam into each indentation.

Bake for 20 minutes, rotating the baking sheet halfway through, until golden around the edges.

Let cool on the baking sheet for 10 minutes and serve warm, or let cool completely and store in an airtight container at room temperature for 5 days or in the freezer for up to 2 months.

ANISE BISCOTTI

MAKES 25 COOKIES

113 g (½ cup) unsalted butter, plus more for the pan

165 g (¾ cup) sugar

4 g (1 tsp) anise seeds

15 g (1 Tbsp) Grand Marnier liqueur

5 g (1 tsp) orange-flower water

6 g (1 Tbsp) fresh orange zest

100 g (2 large) eggs

365 g (2½ cups) sifted heritage flour (SWS), such as White Sonora

5 g (1 tsp) baking powder

3 g (½ tsp) fine sea salt

75 g (¾ cup) toasted sliced almonds

I love coffee, but I prefer this biscotti with a little tea, especially to complement the anise and orange flavors. Note that making these biscotti requires a two-step baking process. You can find orange-flower water at natural and specialty groceries as well as high-end spice and liquor stores. Omit if you can't find it.

Preheat the oven to 325°F [160°C]. Butter a large rimmed baking sheet or line with a silicone baking mat.

In the bowl of a stand mixer fitted with the paddle attachment, beat the butter and sugar on low speed for 2 to 3 minutes, or until creamy. Add the anise seeds, Grand Marnier, orange-flower water, and orange zest and mix until combined. With the mixer running on low speed, add the eggs, one at a time, and mix until combined. Scrape down the bowl.

In a medium bowl, stir together the flour, baking powder, salt, and almonds, then gradually add to the butter-egg mixture and mix until there are no visible traces of flour. The dough will be dry and slightly sticky; do not overmix.

Divide the dough in half and place on the prepared baking sheet. With your hands, form 2 flat logs that are each 10 by 4 in [25 by 12 cm] and ¾ in [2 cm] tall. Arrange the logs so that they are parallel to each other, spacing them at least 3 in [7.5 cm] apart to allow them to spread during baking.

Bake for 24 minutes, or until light golden brown. Let cool on the baking sheet for 30 minutes. Carefully transfer the logs to a cutting board and cut into ¾-in [2-cm] slices. If the logs crack as you transfer them, don't panic; just cut the cracked part off.

Continued . . .

Lower the oven to 300°F [150°C].

Arrange the cut biscotti on the baking sheet and bake for 15 minutes, or until light golden brown. Let cool completely on the baking sheet before serving. Store the biscotti in an airtight container at room temperature for 10 days, or freeze for up to 2 months. To thaw, leave the biscotti on the counter until they reach room temperature.

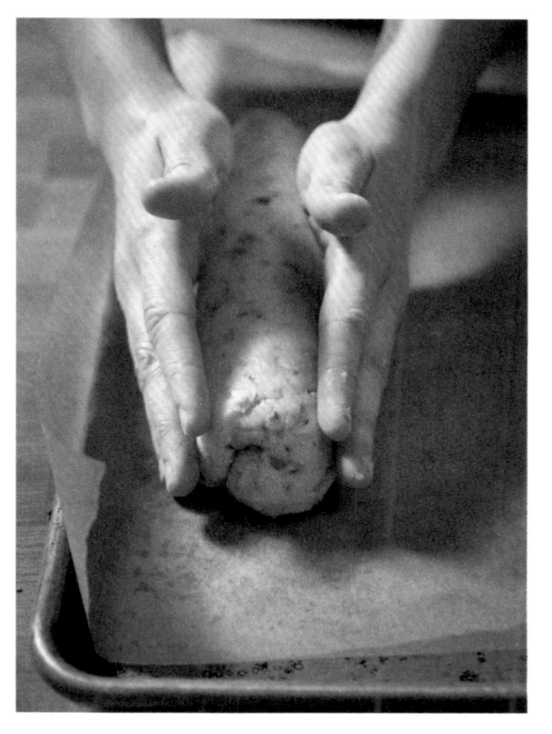

CHOCOLATE-HAZELNUT BISCOTTI

MAKES 12 BISCOTTI

75 g (½ cup) hazelnuts

225 g (1 cup) sugar

113 g (½ cup) unsalted butter, plus 30 g (2 Tbsp)

250 g (1¾ cups) sifted heritage flour (HRW/HRS), such as Rouge de Bordeaux

70 g (½ cup) Dutch-processed cocoa powder

10 g (2 tsp) baking powder

3 g (½ tsp) fine sea salt

2 g (1 tsp) freshly grated orange zest

100 g (2 large) eggs

20 g (2 Tbsp) amaretto liqueur

75 g (⅓ cup plus 1 Tbsp) dark chocolate chips

Our customers love biscotti, so we decided to come up with a rich chocolate biscotti that pairs well with espresso. This is one of our most popular biscotti cookies; it's hard to keep enough of it in stock. Once baked, the cookies will last for a couple of weeks in an airtight container.

Preheat the oven to 350°F [175°C]. Spread the hazelnuts out on a rimmed baking sheet and toast for 8 to 10 minutes, or until golden and fragrant. Line a baking sheet with a silicone baking mat or parchment paper.

While the nuts toast, heat 75 g [⅓ cup] of the sugar in a small saucepan over medium heat, stirring occasionally, until the sugar melts and becomes a light-golden brown caramel, 3 to 4 minutes. Transfer the hazelnuts from the oven to the pan. Turn off the heat and stir to coat. Add the 30 g [2 Tbsp] butter and stir to coat completely.

Pour the caramel-nut mixture onto the prepared baking sheet and let cool completely. Coarsely chop and set aside.

Turn the oven to 325°F [160°C]. Butter a large rimmed baking sheet or line with a silicone baking mat.

In a large bowl, mix the flour, cocoa, baking powder, and salt.

In the bowl of a stand mixer fitted with the paddle attachment, beat the remaining 113 g [½ cup] butter, remaining 150 g [¾ cup] sugar, and the orange zest on low speed for about 2 minutes, or until creamy. Scrape down the bowl. With the mixer running on low speed, add the eggs, one at a time, followed by the amaretto, and mix until combined. Scrape down the bowl again.

Continued . . .

Add the dry ingredients, the chocolate chips, and the chopped praline and mix just until incorporated. Divide the dough into 2 logs and place parallel to each other on the prepared baking sheets, leaving 3 to 4 in [7.5 to 10 cm] of space between each log to allow room for spreading during baking. Shape and pat down each log until it measures 10 by 4 in [25 by 12 cm] and ¾ in [2 cm] tall.

Bake for 25 minutes, rotating the pan halfway through, until the top and sides are lightly colored. Let cool on the baking sheet for 30 minutes. Carefully transfer the logs to a cutting board and cut into 1-in [2.5-cm] slices. If the logs crack as you transfer them, don't panic; just cut the cracked part off.

Lower the oven to 300°F [150°C].

Arrange the cut biscotti on the baking sheet and bake for 30 minutes, or until each piece is baked through. The drier each piece, the longer the shelf life it will have. Let cool completely on the baking sheet before serving. Store the biscotti in an airtight container at room temperature for up to 2 weeks, or freeze for up to 2 months. To thaw, leave the biscotti on the counter until they reach room temperature.

HERITAGE DARK CHOCOLATE BROWNIES

MAKES 26 BROWNIES

- 450 g (2 cups) unsalted butter
- 285 g (2 cups) Dutch-processed cocoa powder
- 450 g (9 large) eggs
- 800 g (3¾ cups) sugar
- 4 g (1 tsp) pure vanilla extract
- 290 g (2 cups) sifted heritage flour (HRW/HRS), such as Rouge de Bordeaux
- 4 g (1½ Tbsp) finely ground espresso beans
- 3 g (½ tsp) fine sea salt

These brownies are so rich and chocolaty you literally cannot eat more than one. It might sound strange to add whole-wheat flour to a brownie recipe, but the Rouge de Bordeaux is a delicate variety that adds earthy flavor rather than density, especially when paired with the jolt of espresso. I use European-style or Dutch-processed cocoa powder because the Dutch processing removes acidity from the cocoa for a smoother flavor.

Preheat the oven to 350°F [175°C]. Line a 9-by-13-in [23-by-33-cm] baking pan with parchment paper and coat the parchment with cooking spray.

Combine the butter and cocoa powder in a double boiler or a metal heatproof bowl set over a saucepan filled with 1 in [2.5 cm] of simmering water, making sure that the water does not touch the bottom of the bowl. Cook, stirring, until all the butter is melted and the cocoa powder and butter become a liquid; it will become very thick and heavy, so be sure to stir from the bottom to incorporate the butter and cocoa.

In the bowl of a stand mixer fitted with the paddle attachment, or using a handheld mixer and a large bowl, beat the eggs and sugar on low speed until combined. With the mixer running on low speed, slowly pour in the cocoa mixture and vanilla. Add the flour, espresso powder, and salt to the batter and mix until combined.

Pour the batter into the prepared pan, smooth the top, and bake for 30 minutes. Rotate the pan and bake for 10 minutes more, or until the top is dry and a metal skewer or toothpick inserted into the center comes out with moist crumbs. Be careful not to overbake.

Let the brownies cool completely in the pan before cutting into squares. Serve or store in an airtight container at room temperature for 4 days or freeze brownie squares in a resealable plastic bag for up to 2 months. To thaw, let sit on the counter at room temperature for 2 hours or warm in a 325°F [160°C] oven for 10 minutes.

RASPBERRY MASCARPONE BROWNIES

MAKES 26 BROWNIES

- 1 recipe Heritage Dark Chocolate Brownie batter (page 214), prepared up to the point that it is poured in the pan
- 225 g (1 cup) mascarpone cheese
- 55 g (¼ cup) sugar
- 50 g (1 large) egg
- 36 g (¼ cup) sifted heritage flour (SRS), such as White Sonora or Richland
- 160 g (½ cup) your favorite homemade or store-bought raspberry or plum jam

This is a variation of our dark brownie recipe. When trying to decide on a new brownie recipe, we all voted and this was the clear winner. Our customers quickly became addicted to it. I recommend making the jam-cheese filling before you make the batter because if the brownies sit too long after being poured in the pan, they can turn into concrete before baking.

Preheat the oven to 350°F [175°C]. Line a 9-by-13-in [23-by-33-cm] baking pan with parchment paper and coat the parchment with cooking spray.

Pour the brownie batter into the prepared pan and smooth the top.

In a medium bowl, stir together the mascarpone cheese, sugar, and egg with a wooden spoon until well combined. Add the flour and stir until creamy.

Dollop tablespoonfuls of the mascarpone mixture on top of the brownie batter, spacing the dollops 2 in [5 cm] apart.

Using a spoon, drizzle the jam over the mascarpone, then lightly swirl it into the batter with a knife, barely touching the top of the jam so it stays on the surface.

Bake for 40 minutes, rotating the pan halfway through, or until a metal skewer or toothpick inserted into the middle comes out with moist crumbs.

Let the brownies cool completely in the pan before cutting into squares. Serve or store in an airtight container at room temperature for 4 days or freeze brownie squares in a resealable plastic bag for up to 2 months. To thaw, let sit on the counter at room temperature for 2 hours or warm in a 325°F [160°C] oven for 10 minutes.

ACKNOWLEDGMENTS

THE FIRST TIME I THOUGHT about writing a cookbook was during my years as a graduate student at the University of Maine. After researching classic colonial dishes, I soon realized that this could be a terrible idea! Who would want to eat this food? Yet if I had ventured further to research colonial baking recipes, I might have been more inspired. The way we bake at Hewn is the same way our ancestors baked bread and other baked goods so many years ago, before commercial baking and the commodity flour industry took hold. Many of us go out of our way to connect with local farmers and shop for heirloom produce and meat and eggs from well-cared-for animals. The time for this type of cookbook, one that brings us back to our roots when it comes to growing wheat and milling flour—a classically American tradition—is here.

Thank you to Amelia Levin, my collaborator on this project, who helped me realize that our conversation about heritage baking was more than just a magazine article—that it could make for a great cookbook. And thank you to my agent, Jenni-Ferrari Adler, for believing in our ideas and connecting us with the right publisher.

That said, a huge thanks to Sarah Billingsley, our fantastic editor on the book. We have valued your precision, patience, support, and guidance along the way. Thank you, also, to our fantastic photographer, John Lee, for capturing the beauty of heritage wheat, along with the farmers who grow it and the millers who mill it. And, of course, thank you for making the beauty of our breads and pastries really shine.

This book would not be possible without all the amazing people who make up Hewn. First, I would like to thank Justin Holmes, our head baker, who took a chance and moved to Chicago when Hewn was nothing more than an idea. Thank you for uprooting your life to work at Hewn and for your tremendous dedication, calm demeanor, and sense of humor. Thank you to Spencer Hendrickson, who makes the pastry side shine and seem so easy. Thank you to Timmy Gibbons and Sam Campbell for your diligent testing and commitment. Thank you to members of our talented baking team who allowed me time to work on this book: Josh Axler, Joe Falcinelli, John Snyder, Anton Gadbois, and Leah Leman.

Many thanks to our additional group of testers: Kaitlyn Gilham, Maggie Schmidt, Dawn Patch, Tracy Leman, and Erin Quaglia. Thank you to Hannah Ross for her creativity. We are so grateful for your hard work and dedication.

I have so many people to thank for helping me find my way before Hewn took off. Being a historian, I'll go back to the beginning. My parents stuck by me and always believed in me, even when I made really bad decisions. My mom always encouraged me to move forward and be positive, and I owe her for giving me my first baking book, which inspired my bread-baking hobby-turned-business. Thank you also to my dad, who passed away before he could see how my professional culinary career evolved. I learned so much from his experiences working in food, back when it was just called food service. He would have loved Hewn, and I often think of him when I'm alone at the bakery. Thanks also to my two brothers, Jon and Tim, for their continued support and encouragement over the years.

I would also like to thank my favorite teacher from Naperville North High School, Mrs. (Holly) Lee, who sent me on my path of studying history. Mrs. Lee allowed me into her AP European history course, even with my miserable GPA. I am forever grateful for her guidance and willingness to take a chance on me. She taught me to love history, and I learned how to put current events into a historical perspective. Most importantly, she challenged me to be a better student and person and to never stop asking why.

I was fortunate enough to attend the Seattle Culinary Academy. Thank you to all of the chefs who taught me: Chef Miyata, Chef Madayag, Chef Dillard, and especially Chef Don Reed, for introducing me to bread and baking with a wood-fired oven at Quillisascut Farmstead Cheese School.

I would also like to thank Thierry Rautereau for allowing "Hellen" to learn and work in his kitchen when I was more of a liability than an asset. Thank you to Andrew Will, who taught me how to maintain really high standards. I would also like to thank Alice Gautsch and the Seattle chapter of Les Dames d'Escoffier for their support after awarding me with a scholarship to attend culinary school. Thank you to Leslie Mackie of Macrina Bakery for always being so generous with your time and for patiently and thoughtfully answering all of my questions.

To my Underground Bread Club members: you helped me create this business, and without your early support, Hewn would not exist. A special thanks to my original club members Rick Boynton, Kim Cohen, Stephanie Michel, Tracy Gallun, Mary-Kay Halston, and Amanda Hyslop. Thanks, also, to Laurie Olsen-Perkins for your insight, support, and advice over the years.

To my son, Asher, thank you for putting up with my long hours at the bakery and for having to hang out there while I worked. Thank you, also, for being my first salesperson and for graciously helping me cart loaves of bread around town and to school. You are my best taste tester and I love you very much!

Last but never least, a huge thank-you to Julie Matthei, my wonderful business and life partner. Without your balanced and calm approach to the business—and to our lives—Hewn and our relationship would not have lasted.

INDEX

HEWN